OXFORD ENGLISH FOR CAREERS

COMMERCE

Martyn Hobbs and Julia Starr Keddle

Teacher's Resource Book

OXFORD
UNIVERSITY PRESS

OXFORD
UNIVERSITY PRESS

Great Clarendon Street, Oxford OX2 6DP

Oxford University Press is a department of the University of Oxford.
It furthers the University's objective of excellence in research, scholarship,
and education by publishing worldwide in

Oxford New York

Auckland Cape Town Dar es Salaam Hong Kong Karachi
Kuala Lumpur Madrid Melbourne Mexico City Nairobi
New Delhi Shanghai Taipei Toronto

With offices in

Argentina Austria Brazil Chile Czech Republic France Greece
Guatemala Hungary Italy Japan Poland Portugal Singapore
South Korea Switzerland Thailand Turkey Ukraine Vietnam

OXFORD and OXFORD ENGLISH are registered trade marks of
Oxford University Press in the UK and in certain other countries

ISBN: 978 0 19 456985 9

Printed in China

ACKNOWLEDGEMENTS

Artwork sourced by Pictureresearch.co.uk

*We would also like to thank the following for permission to reproduce the
following photographs:*
Alamy pp 81 (jet/Antony Nettle), 83 (escalators/Robert Stainforth),
91 (office/top. l/ImageState), 91 (office/top. r/Lourens Smak),
91 (office/bot. l/Bill Varie); Corbis pp 81 (home/Roy Botterell),
81 (cars/Keren Su); 83 (chips/Steve Prezant); Getty Images pp 72 (Adrian
Weinbrecht/Iconica), 73 (Matt/Robb Kendrick), 73 (Lucia/Phil Boorman/The
Image Bank), 75 (computers/Thomas Lohnes/AFP); Punchstock pp 73
(Katrina/Andrew Wakeford/Digital Vision), 73 (Alberto/Thinkstock),
75 (logs/John Foxx/Stockbyte), 75 (cars/Hans-Peter Merten/Digital Vision),
77 (Image Source), 81 (internet/Goodshoot), 83 (checkout/Digital Vision),
91 (office/bot. r/Brand X Pictures), 95 (Jose Luis Pelaez Inc/Blend Images),
99 (Tom Le Goff/Digital Vision), 101 (Tom Le Goff/Digital Vision)

Contents

Introduction

Commerce is designed for students who intend to get a job in a business context. It prepares them for a wide range of business situations, develops telephone and communication skills, and provides them with a background in major business concepts.

Start up

This is designed as a warm-up activity to the unit. It often introduces key vocabulary or concepts, and should be used to get students to focus on the topic.

Meeting room

'Meeting room' is set in the offices of a magazine publisher with regular characters – Laura, Kim, Jamie, and Yusuf. It presents the functional language that students need to interact effectively in more formal business situations such as meetings. Areas include giving opinions, adding and contrasting information, explaining, and turn-taking. There are listening tasks after which students are asked to analyse the interaction. Students are then required to do speaking tasks and role plays that practise the language in meaningful contexts. These are linked to Pronunciation exercises where necessary.

Small talk

This section alternates with 'Meeting room' and has two regular characters, Karen and Daniel, who interact with their colleagues. It deals with the social and conversational 'micro-functions' that occur between colleagues at their desks, in the canteen, round the water cooler, etc. Socializing is often neglected in the teaching of business English, but it is essential for effective communication in a professional environment. Areas include making requests, interrupting, making suggestions, and gaining thinking time. The section is organized in the same way as 'Meeting room'.

It's my job / Company profile

These occur in alternate units, and provide visual input and text. They are all based on authentic interviews and sources and are designed to be of interest to the students as they stand with only minimal tasks. In 'It's my job', students will read about a variety of young people in different business environments and gain insight into the skills required.

General focus questions for 'It's my job' and 'Company profile' are: *What do you think his / her job involves? What skills and experience does he / she need? Would you like to do it? What do you know about this company? Would you like to work there?*

As an ongoing project, encourage the class to build up a portfolio of other 'It's my job' or 'Company profile' features.

Business know-how

Increasingly in business, it is not enough to have experience or qualifications. Employers are also looking for staff with strongly developed soft skills. These skills include teamwork skills, self motivation, flexibility, leadership skills, organizational skills, and interpersonal skills. This section is designed to introduce these skills gently to the students through entertaining activities.

Project

This encourages students to take an active role in the learning process, working in pairs or groups to explore topics and find out more about companies.

Projects can be set as homework assignments, but it is worth spending time in class preparing students for the task. Students are usually required to use search engines such as www.google.com or www.altavista.com to find information. Help can also be given by brainstorming some standard places where they can gather information.

Top margin

This part of the page contains facts, statistics, and quotes. These are optional extras and can be used to add variety and interest to your lessons, or provide additional material for strong students who are 'fast finishers'.

Sometimes they have an associated question, and ways of exploitation include asking whether your students are surprised by the facts and statistics, or whether they agree, disagree, or can identify with the quotes.

There are also definitions for difficult words or phrases which are important to understand a text which appears on the same page. (Words or phrases in the text are highlighted in bold.)

Vocabulary

Students meet a large amount of vocabulary during the course. It is important to encourage good learning skills from the start, for example:

● organizing vocabulary into categories rather than simple alphabetical lists

● understanding the context of vocabulary and whether it is a key word needed for production or for comprehension

● checking and learning the pronunciation of a word or phrase.

Language spot

This focuses on the grammar that is generated by the topic of the unit and concentrates on its practical application.

If your students need revision after completing the Language spot, direct them to the Grammar reference, which provides a handy check.

There is also one photocopiable Grammar test for each unit in this Teacher's Resource Book.

Listening, Reading, Speaking, Writing

These activities give realistic and communicative practice of language skills needed in commerce.

● In the listening activities students are exposed to business situations, including dialogues, presentations, and interviews. They also hear a variety of English accents, both native-speaker and non-native speaker.

● In the reading sections students meet a variety of business-based texts.

● In the speaking sections, try to ensure use of English during speaking activities, particularly those involving some discussion. Encourage this by teaching or revising any functional language students may need. The Photocopiable activities in this Teacher's Resource Book also provide additional, freer discussion activities.

● Writing practice in the units is designed as consolidation and extension of the topic with structured, meaningful writing tasks (see Writing bank).

Pronunciation

This practises aspects of pronunciation which are of maximum importance for intelligibility.

You can repeat the recordings in the Pronunciation as often as you like until you and your students feel confident they have mastered a particular sound or feature.

Checklist

This allows students to check their own progress. You may want to get students to grade or assess how well they can perform each of the 'Can do' statements, e.g. 'easily', 'with difficulty', or 'not at all'.

Key words

These are the main items of commerce vocabulary introduced in the unit. A definition of each of these words appears in the Glossary. Students may want to transfer some of the words to their Vocabulary notebook. You should certainly check students' pronunciation, including the stress, of words likely to be used orally.

This section also provides students with the opportunity to personalize the Key words by adding five more words or phrases that they think are useful.

Writing bank

This is in the middle of the book and gives specific skills practice in basic business writing. It can be used throughout the course, either in class, or as self-study or homework. There are recommendations for when to use the different exercises in the teaching notes in this Teacher's Resource Book. There is also an Answer key in the Student's Book to encourage students to check their work, but it is important for you to check extended written answers with reference to the models provided.

Speaking activities

This section contains one or more parts of the information gap activities from the main units (see Speaking).

Grammar reference

This can be used together with the Language spot, as a handy check or revision. It shows the form of a particular grammar point, briefly explains its use, and provides example sentences as well as indicating likely student errors.

Listening scripts

This is a complete transcript of all the recordings. Direct students to it for checking answers after they have completed a Listening task, or allow weaker students to read it as they listen to a particular recording, perhaps for a final time.

Glossary

This is an alphabetical list of all the Key words. Each word is followed by the pronunciation in phonetic script, the part of speech, and a definition in English.

The section begins with a phonetic chart, with an example word from commerce to illustrate each of the sounds.

1 New jobs

Background

In 2006, a survey was conducted of human resource officials in the US. It aimed to discover the views of employers on the readiness of high school and college graduates to enter the workplace. The report concluded that they believed that young people were not prepared for the transition from full-time education to work. Where employers expected their new employees to have a range of basic knowledge and interpersonal skills, their new intake didn't meet their expectations.

On the academic front, the most significant problem was writing. Nearly 75% of graduate employees were viewed as being deficient in basic writing skills such as grammar and spelling. This deficiency was also reflected in their inability to apply these skills to practical work-based communications including letter-writing, emails, memos and reports.

Furthermore, the survey revealed that employers placed even more emphasis on essential soft skills. To survive in the workplace, employees need 'practical abilities' such as time-management, teamwork, prioritizing, etc. Employers believed that nearly three quarters of their new intake fell below acceptable levels. Clearly, these are areas in which students need preparation – and these skills can be learned.

However, the picture isn't entirely negative! The new generation of employees comes with an array of skills that their older colleagues do not possess. Young people today starting work come with enormous technological experience. It has been estimated that a typical 21-year-old would have already exchanged 250,000 emails, instant messages and text messages; spent 10,000 hours on mobile phones; played video games for 5,000 hours, and spent 3,500 hours online. Even taking variations between the young people of different countries, it's clear that the digital generation are at home with new technologies where 30- and 40-year-olds are less at ease. Although young employees lack essential basic academic and soft skills, they do bring other abilities to the workplace.

➕ Additional activity

(all levels)
Students can write a paragraph about their first day.

✳ Tip

gossip informal talk or stories about other people's private lives
deadlines a point in time when something must be done

Start up

1 Get students to discuss a first day somewhere (a workplace, new school, etc.). Ask some pairs to tell the class their stories.

2 Ask students to read 'First day nerves' and discuss the questions: *How should you behave? How should you dress?* Ask students to read through the advice and decide which are dos and don'ts. Write *Dos* and *Don'ts* on the board and get students to come up and put their advice in the correct column. Get students to explain their reasons.

> **⚷ Possible answers**
>
> **Do**
> - smile and be friendly
> - introduce yourself to everyone
> - learn the names of your colleagues
> - volunteer for projects
> - arrive at work on time
> - ask questions
> - stick to deadlines
>
> **Don't**
> - learn all the office gossip
> - compare the new job with your old one
> - refuse offers of help (*it's OK to need help, you won't look stupid and it will help you get to know people*)
> - leave on time
> - wear casual clothes
> - stick to your lunch hour

3 Divide the students into small groups to discuss the advice. Go through their ideas at class level.

Reading

1 Discuss the photo with the students – ask them *Who is she talking to? How do you think she feels?* Then ask students to scan the article and find the points from *Start up*.

> 🔑 being smart, walk in with a smile, be polite and friendly, introduce yourself, learn names of colleagues, don't be afraid to ask questions, arrive early, leave no earlier than the majority, don't get involved in office gossip

2 Ask students to scan the article again and find the opposites of the adjectives. Do the first one together with the class.

> 🔑 casual – smart, disorganized – organized, unreliable – reliable, easy – difficult, confident – nervous, negative – positive

3 Before reading, go through the items and ask students to guess the answers. Then get them to read the article and check their guesses.

> 🔑 1 it tells people you are organized and reliable.   2 people remember what you say when you are new.   3 it is better to ask than make mistakes.   4 you don't have to keep asking the same questions. 5 every company has its own way of doing things.   6 it doesn't make a good impression.   7 it may stop people trusting you.   8 you will get to know them.

Vocabulary

Business sectors

Go through the Business sectors with the students, checking they understand what happens in each one. In pairs, get students to think of five words for each one. Encourage students to think of words they already know, and re-use words for different sectors, such as *manager*. Ask students if they would like to work in any of the sectors.

> 🔑 **Possible answers**
> banking – bank, cashier, bank manager, account, investment, loan, online banking, transfer, payment, balance, accounting
> catering – food, chef, waiter, table, menu, buffet, events, airlines, service, hospitality
> publishing – books, magazines, printing, literature, information, electronic media, printing press, editor, writer, reader
> tourism – holiday, package, travel agent, travel, leisure, tourist, hotel, airlines, tour guide, transportation,
> advertising – sell, ideas, advertising executive, creatives, advertising agency, client, designer, promotion, advert, TV commercial
> retail – shops, department stores, shop assistant, customer, buyer, goods, sell, buy, consumer

➕ Additional activity

(stronger students)
Ask students to work in the same groups as in exercise 3, page 4. Ask them to compare the points they chose with the points mentioned in the article. Now they have read the article would they change the points they chose?

➕ Additional activity

(stronger students)
After doing exercise 2 get students to cover the article. Get them to do exercise 3 without looking at the article.

✳ Tip

Top margin p.6
Ask students to read the stories. Ask them to vote on which story they think is the most embarrassing.

➕ Additional activity

(weaker students)
Ask students to write a sentence for some of their words, e.g. *Accessories are items such as belts, hats and jewellery.*

➕ Additional activity

(stronger students)
Students can go online and find these and other job sectors in job search sites.
www.totaljobs.com ; www.jobserve.com.
Ask them to explore the jobs available for one of the sectors.

* Tip

Collocations
deal with mail / emails / money
have a meeting / have lunch
arrive in the office / get to my desk /
work late / work on research / a project etc.

➕ Additional activity

(weaker students)
Instead of the reading exercise, get
students to read both texts in pairs and
complete the table together. Then check
the answers with students at class level.

➕ Additional activity

(all levels)
Get students to cover the reading texts
and answer the questions.
*Who ... has worked in the job for two
months? answers the phone a lot? answers
letters in the afternoon? meets sellers and
looks at products? is trying to improve his
or her typing? works until 6.30? deals with
emails before he or she goes home? found
the first day stressful?*

➕ Photocopiable activity
First day
Go to p.73 Teacher's Resource Book.

* Tip

mail shot advertising sent to a large
number of people at the same time
people skills the ability to deal with people
well

Reading

Before looking at the *Reading*, ask students to tell you what assistants and
fashion buyers do each day.

Ask students to work in pairs. Each student only reads about one person.
Get them to complete the table for the person they are reading about. Then
get students to ask and answer questions in pairs, including the parts of the
table which were already filled in. Round up at class level.

Ask students to look at the texts again and describe Emma and Hugo's first
day in the job.

O┰ Emma:

typical morning routine: deal with mail, have a meeting with boss, answer
the phone, run errands

lunch: at desk, reading magazines

typical afternoon routine: different projects, send documents, answer
readers' letters

at the moment: working on the letters page, researching an article on
'How to save time', trying to improve typing skills

Hugo:
how long in the job: two months

typical morning routine: check email and voicemail, write sales report and
send to boss, receive consignments of sample clothes

lunch: sandwich at desk

typical afternoon routine: varied, sometimes meets sellers and looks at
products

at the moment: collecting samples for a photo shoot, preparing the
catalogue for next year

before going home: deals with outstanding emails

Listening

Ask students what they think happens at a business centre that arranges
conferences.

Go through the questions and then play the recording and ask students to
make notes. Get them to check the answers in pairs and then listen again.

Get students to work in pairs and role play the conversation between the
interviewer and Caroline.

O┰ 1 helps to staff the reception desk
2 answer the phone, book clients into the office, deal with enquiries, do a
lot of office tasks, use the computer, fax and photocopy documents,
prepare presentations, take post to the post office
3 working with colleague Jenny preparing promotional mail shots,
writing copy and updating client mailing lists
4 working in a team and meeting new people
5 being patient, having good people skills, not getting stressed
6 sat next to a colleague and watched

➕ Grammar test

Go to p.72 Teacher's Resource Book.

➕ Additional activity

(weaker students)

In pairs get students to discuss:

● a typical day at work / school / college
● what they are doing at work / in their studies at the moment
● what they do just before they go home.

The first and last points require students to use the Present Simple. The middle one requires the Present Continuous. Ask students to write one paragraph for each topic.

✳ Tip

Away Day an all day meeting for a team, away from the normal office environment. It is designed to look at how the business is working, develop new strategies, think creatively about the business, and team build.

Language spot
Present Simple v Present Continuous

Ask students to read the examples and complete the rules. Go through the Grammar reference with the students or set for homework.

> **O⚷** Use the Present Simple for things that are generally true and facts.
> Use the Present Continuous to talk about things that are happening now.
> Use the Present Simple to talk about daily routines and situations that exist over a long period of time.
> Use the Present Continuous to talk about temporary events or situations that are happening over a limited period of time.

Ask students to complete the email.

> **O⚷** 1 am writing   2 allows   3 work   4 deal   5 answer
> 6 am learning   7 ask   8 hope   9 like   10 go   11 is
> 12 is walking

Meeting room
Agreeing and disagreeing

1 Ask students to speculate about the picture: *What sort of company is it? What is the relationship between the people?* etc. Play the recording and ask students to note what the people do.

> **O⚷** Laura, manager; Kim, editorial assistant; Jamie, head of production; Yusuf, head of sales and marketing.

2 Go through the questions, then play the recording and get students to answer the questions.

> **O⚷** 1 arrange an Away Day to have a team-building session
> 2 They're very busy. They have lots of new staff. It's important they get to know each other   3 Kim: half a day instead of a day

3 Go through the *Expressions* list. Play the recording and get students to tick the phrases they hear. Get students to repeat them after you or after the recording, then copy them into their notebook.

> **O⚷** I'm thinking of...   I think it's important...   I'm hoping...
> Yes, that's a good idea.   That's true.   (Laura's) You're absolutely right.
> I'm not sure about that.

Speaking

Go through the *Expressions* list with the students. Ask them to repeat the sentences after you, paying attention to pronunciation and intonation. Divide the class into groups of three. Tell students to read their role cards. They then do one activity at a time discussing the situations. Encourage students to use the expressions from *Meeting room*. Go round the class checking their progress and dealing with any errors.

∗ Tip

Top margin p.8
Ask students to read the quote and look at the picture. *Why is 'Vogue' like heaven for David Bailey? Which magazine might represent heaven for them?*

➕ Additional activity
(all levels)
Extra questions for Reading
Where is Condé Nast based? What is the readership of Glamour, or GQ? When was Condé Nast founded? What happened in the 1990s? What did Steve Florio do? What was the profit in 1996? What is CondeNet? How do you get a job at Condé Nast?

∗ Tip

This *Business know-how* is designed to get students and you talking about time management and ways in which you can focus on your work. Provide opportunities for students to share their ideas and discuss their experiences. If possible, tell them of your own experiences (positive and negative) in time management.

➕ Writing bank
CV1
Go to p.63 Student's Book.

➕ Additional activity
(weaker students)
Ask students to answer these questions about the personal profile:
What are Giulio's hobbies and interests? What is he good at? What has he done for a free paper? What is he studying for? What is his English like? How would he like to improve his English?

Company profile
Condé Nast

1 Ask students to work in pairs and think about all the things which they have read in the past week. To help them, tell them some of the things you have read. Get students to discuss the questions. Discuss them at class level.

2 Ask students to read *Company profile* and answer the questions.

> **⊙↦** 1 30 2 Condé Montrose Nast 3 S.I Newhouse's Advance Publications
> 4 London, Paris, Milan 5 energetic with strong people skills
> 6 editorial (developing magazines), corporate (accounting, manufacturing, public relations, market research), advertising (merchandising and promoting), online (websites)

Project

Individually or in pairs, get students to choose a magazine (preferably English) and write a short report on it, focusing on the questions. If possible, they should buy it to get information, and find out about it online. If time, get students to give presentations to the class about their project.

Business know-how

1 In pairs, get students to discuss the question. Round up the discussion at class level.

2 In pairs, get students to read the tips. Ask them to compare their ideas with the tips. Each student can choose a technique to focus on. Throughout the year, refer back to this advice to help students organize their study time.

Writing

1 Go through the instructions with the students and discuss the role of a personal profile. Ask them to read the profile and match the headings with the paragraphs. Explain, if necessary, that the ECDL is a qualification in computer skills which is recognised throughout Europe.

> **⊙↦** Paragraph 1: Sector I am interested in
> Paragraph 2: Relevant hobbies and interests
> Paragraph 3: Skills and qualities
> Paragraph 4: Experience, qualifications and training
> Paragraph 5: Language ability
> Paragraph 6: Goals and ambitions

2 Explain to students that personal profiles can help them gather together information about themselves, their skills and experience. They should regard a personal profile as something that they start in this unit, but that they come back to and rewrite during the course, and during their career. Ask students to make notes under the headings. Then get them to write their own personal profile, using the text as a model.

2 Buying and selling

Background

Without markets, businesses couldn't function. A **market** is where people who want to sell can do business with people who want to buy. In traditional markets, people set up stalls and sell their products directly to consumers. Contemporary British variations on this model are farmers' markets and car boot sales. But there are in fact thousands of different kinds of markets for specific purposes. As the buyers and sellers are scattered over the whole world, in most cases they don't physically meet. So while markets can exist in physical places, such as the Stock Exchange, they can also be 'invisible' with transactions carried out via the telephone, email and the Internet.

The four main types are **commodity markets** for the buying and selling of goods such as gas, precious metals and coffee; **consumer markets**, where retailers can sell to the general public; **industrial markets**, where businesses trade with other business, not with a final consumer; and **capital markets**. Here, businesses can 'buy' money in the form of shares and bonds.

The **price** of goods and services is determined by market forces and depends on the relationship between the **supply** of goods and the **demand** for them. When supply is greater than demand, producers will reduce production and lower prices. Where demand outstrips supply, producers will increase production and raise prices.

All businesses can be grouped into three interdependent sectors, depending on their main activity.

- The primary sector involves the production and collection of raw materials.
- The secondary sector includes businesses that manufacture or construct goods.
- The tertiary sector provides services to businesses and consumers.

These sectors are all linked in a chain of production. For example, in the case of a magazine, the primary sector is involved in the felling of trees. The secondary sector is responsible for the manufacturing of paper and the production of the finished item. The magazine is then distributed by the tertiary sector, including transporters, wholesalers and retailers (in shops and online), and banks (to process payments).

Start up

1 Get students to work in small groups and discuss the list. Go through the pronunciation of any problematic words. When they have discussed all the items on the list they should choose the five they consider most necessary. Round up at class level and decide on a class list of five items.

2 Discuss at class level with students what they think are the basic necessities to everyday life, such as water, food, shelter.

➕ Additional activity

(all levels)
Ask students to decide individually the buying habit they have which is most related to wants, e.g. CDs, clothes, shoes, mobile phones, etc.

Reading

1 Refer back to the list in *Start up*. Ask students if they need CDs or want them. They may argue that people don't need CDs or downloadable music but that they need music in their lives in some way. Allow the discussion to develop in this way, so that you can decide together the basics of life. Then ask students to read the article and answer the questions. Ask students to think of examples of how we meet the needs in our daily lives and when a need becomes a want.

2 Get students to work in pairs and discuss the questions. Each individual will have a different attitude and experience of meeting needs and wants. But most students will have some 'wants' which are not really necessary to life.

➕ Additional activity

(weaker students)

Ask students to write their answers to question 3 for homework.

➕ Grammar test

Go to p.74 Teacher's Resource Book.

✳ Tip

Useful expressions for telling a story

Opening

I had an interesting / embarrassing / exciting / strange experience.

When I was about twenty …

When I started my new job …

I was working / studying / travelling …

Continuing

Then … So … But … Guess what happened next.

Showing interest

Really? Did you? What happened next? How did you feel?

✳ Tip

Top margin p.12

Get students to read the quotes and say if they agree or disagree with them.

➕ Photocopiable activity

Business activities

Go to p.75 Teacher's Resource Book.

✳ Tip

bargain something that is bought or sold at a lower price

supply and demand the relationship between the amount of goods and materials that is available and the amount that people want to buy. This affects price.

raw materials a natural or basic substance that is used in an industrial process

market forces things that affect the price of a product or service, the price it should be sold at, and the way it should be sold

➕ Additional activity

(stronger students)

Ask students to write an 80–100 word summary of the article. Advise them to write one sentence for each paragraph, except the last one.

3 Go through the examples with students before they do the task. Get students to answer the questions individually before they discuss their answers together.

Language spot

Past Simple v Past Continuous

Ask students to read the rules and then match the examples with the correct rules.

> **⚷** 1 Hi Sonia. I just got your message. I wasn't at my desk when you called.
> 2 What were you doing? I was reading a report.
> 3 I met my friend Brian while / when I was studying Business at college.
> 4 Hussein was working for an Import-Export company when he moved to Italy in 2006.

Ask students to read the article again and find examples of the Past Continuous and the Past Simple.

Go through the Grammar reference with students or set it as homework.

1 Ask students to complete the text in class or for homework.

> **⚷** 1 was surfing 2 wasn't doing 3 was 4 was looking
> 5 noticed 6 looked 7 was planning 8 thought
> 9 placed 10 was working 11 checked 12 was bidding
> 13 became 14 didn't buy 15 had 16 were talking
> 17 started 18 was wearing

2 Get students to individually prepare for the activity by choosing a topic and making notes. Suggest they think about: *When and where it happened, What was happening at the time, What they felt*. They could then write up their story for homework.

Reading

1 Ask students to look at the pictures and make a note of what they think is being sold in each case.

> **⚷** Picture 1: a house; Picture 2: vegetables; Picture 3: stocks and shares; Picture 4: an online purchase

2 Ask students to tell you what was the last thing they bought. Ask them: *How do you think the price is set for this item?* Ask students to read the article. Ask them this question: *What examples of things that are sold are there in the article?*

Get students to read the article and answer the questions. In pairs, they can discuss their answers. Round up at class level.

1 Sellers want the best price. Buyers want the cheapest price.
2 Students' own answers
3 **Possible answer**
Because they won't be able to sell something if it is much more expensive than similar products, and they won't get a decent return if they price it too low
4 Market forces
5 Producers will lower their prices if the supply is greater than the demand / if there is no interest from buyers.
6 Producers will raise their prices if the demand is greater than the supply / if there is a lot of interest.

3 Ask students to complete the notes.

Buyers: what is available; how desperately I need it; if the price is OK; if there is a better bargain elsewhere; how much time I have got
Sellers: the value of the goods; the price people are prepared to accept; what other sellers are charging; the profit they will make; how much it will cost to produce; the cost of sales and delivery

➕ Additional activity
Get students to use online dictionaries to explore these terms in more depth.

Vocabulary
Economic terms

Get students to match the words and definitions.

goods – d; supply – f; demand – e; services – b; transaction – a; value – c

✳ Tip
Expressions
If there are too many expressions for weaker students, suggest they choose one or two to learn.

✳ Tip
Note the structure of indirect polite questions:
Do you think you could …? NOT *Do you think could you …?*
Would you mind + -ing form
Would you mind if I + past form

Small talk
Requests

1 Ask students to look at the picture and guess what is happening. Then play the recording and get students to make a note of what Karen wants to know. Play the recording again and ask students to make a note of the answers that Karen is given.

1 where the blue meeting room is
2 the number of the IT department
3 the name of the Human Resources Manager
Excuse: the person doesn't know

2 Go through the *Expressions* list and get students to listen again and tick the expressions they hear.

Excuse me.   Sorry, but…   Could you possibly…?   Do you think you could…?   Would you mind telling me…?   Yes, of course.   Not at all.   I'm very sorry, but…

Pronunciation
Polite requests

1 Ask students what makes a request rude or polite in their own language (intonation, voice, body language, etc.). Go through the rules with the students. Then play the recording and ask students to listen and repeat.

2 Play the recording. Stop after each request and elicit answers from the class. Only request 3 is rude and should be refused by the students.

Speaking

1 Go through the *Expressions* list with the students again. Ask them to repeat the sentences after you, paying attention to pronunciation and intonation. In groups, get students to agree on a list of how much trouble / disturbance the requests cause. They need to consider how much effort the person has to make, and how personal the request is.

> **⊙━ Possible answer** (from least to most disturbance caused)
> explain how to get to the meeting   borrow your dictionary
> open the window   turn down your radio   use your mobile phone
> get me a glass of water   borrow £10   buy stamps for me
> borrow your bike   finish my report for me

In pairs, get students to choose an expression and a context for each request and then role play the situations. They should take it in turns to make the requests, refuse / agree to the requests.

2 Divide the class into pairs and ask students to do the role play using expressions they studied and polite intonation. After a short time interrupt and ask some strong pairs to perform their role play, giving them feedback where necessary. Then ask all the pairs to continue.

It's my job

1 Ask students to make a note of the main duties and qualities of a music store manager. Round up at class level, making notes on the board.

2 Ask students to read about Jamie Hughes and find the ideas that are on the board.

3 Discuss the question at class level. Ask students if they would like to work as a music store manager.

Listening

1 Get students to look at the pictures and guess what the people have bought. Then play the recording and make notes of what they bought and why they bought it.

> **⊙━** 1 bought a T-shirt because it's Nike   2 bought pens and notebooks because the price was good   3 bought five CDs because they were on special offer and needed to replace his old cassettes.

2 Get students to work in pairs and discuss the question.

Project

1 Ask students to work in pairs and discuss the questions.

➕ Additional activity

(all levels)
Get students to write up a dialogue based on the Speaking activity in class or for homework.

✱ Tip

What requests are appropriate or inappropriate can be culturally determined. For example in British culture it is reasonably common amongst close colleagues to borrow and lend small amounts of money. *Speaking*, exercise 1 is a useful moment to discuss the cultural implications of the requests.

✱ Tip

Top margin p.14
Ask students to discuss the quotations. Do any of the class have experience working in a shop or retail?

➕ Additional activity

(weaker students)
The first time you ask students to read *It's my job*, ask them to answer these questions:
Is Jamie experienced in being a store manager?
What responsibilities does a store manager have?
Why do you think store managers need the qualities that Jamie mentions?
Why does Jamie love the job?

2 Get students to refer to the factors mentioned in *Reading, Market forces*, in relation to their purchases when they write their report. Suggested layout of the report:
- Name of product
- Price / value for money
- Reason for buying it – need or a want
- Factors influencing the price and availability

Business know-how

1 In pairs get the students to discuss the questions. Discuss students' answers at class level. Having problems with energy levels is a problem for most people, and students or people entering the workplace need to understand what makes them feel energized.

2 Get students to read the tips in pairs and discuss them. Ask them: *Which tips do they find the most helpful? Which things do they do already?*

Writing

1 Read through the instructions and situations with the students checking they understand the task. Students can use some of the expressions from *Small talk*.

2 In pairs, students exchange their emails and answer their partner's emails. Write the following instructions on the board, and ask students to use these in their answers.
- You can't email the office phone list because you deleted it by mistake.
- You are happy to explain about the client database, but you don't have time until tomorrow.
- Say where the group meeting takes place, and ask your partner to tell the group that you can't go to it.
- Explain that you can't provide the report as it contains information confidential to your team.

> **O━ Possible answer:**
> Dear Lisa
> I've lost the office phone list. Do you think you could email me it to me?
> Thanks
> Mario
>
> Dear Mario
> I'm really sorry but I have deleted it by mistake, so I don't have it. Why don't you ask Rebecca?
> All the best
> Lisa

➕ Writing bank
Emails 1 – Ordering
Go to p.53 Student's Book.

➕ Additional activity
(stronger students)
Students can write an email to their partner, inventing a situation, starting an email exchange.

3 Marketing

Background

Different customers have different needs, wants and expectations. In a highly competitive and sophisticated marketplace, it is practically impossible for a company to produce a product that would be suitable for all of them. Therefore, most companies are **market-orientated**. They seek to identify the wants and desires of certain types of consumers, and then to produce the goods or services that would satisfy them.

Marketing is based on the theory that people who are like each other will also buy similar products. In fact, many marketing theorists believe that there is no such thing as a 'market', but only **market segments**. That is because a market consists of so many different types of people that it is impossible to meet all their different needs. In the car market, for example, manufacturers don't attempt to produce one vehicle to satisfy the disparate needs of potential consumers. They identify a particular segment of the market, such as those people who are interested in buying sports cars or family cars, and focus their product and their attention on them. In the segmentation of the consumer market, **buying behaviour, demographic**, and **geographic** factors are extremely important.

Demographic, or personal factors, include:
- age – different generations have different needs
- gender – sex differentiation in spending patterns
- socio-economic group – for example, people with higher incomes and more disposable income will be more interested in luxury goods
- status in family – the 'head of the family' will take key decisions relating to the home

The importance of geographic factors to businesses include:
- location – where people live, whether a town or a region
- language skills – which can affect packaging and information leaflets, especially for foreign markets

Companies also use studies of buying behaviour in order to position their goods. These factors include:
- impulse buying – the making of unplanned purchases
- buying patterns – knowing how, when and where people buy, which products they choose, and how much they spend. By issuing 'loyalty' cards, stores can monitor customer buying habits and target discounts and products on particular groups.

✚ Additional activity
(weaker students)
Go through the questions with the students before doing exercise 1.

✚ Additional activity
(stronger students)
Get students to do a survey of about six students with the questionnaire and then write a simple report on the habits of the class.

✽ Tip

use of prepositions
belong *to* something / someone
be addicted *to* something
keep up *with* someone / something
learn *about* something
find out *about* something
sing along *with* someone / a song
be worried *by* something

Start up

1 The exercise is to get students thinking about their own habits as consumers. Ask students to work in pairs, answer the questions and make notes of their partner's answers. Round up at class level, finding the areas where all the class seem to share the same habits.

2 In groups, students discuss the questions, Ask each group to report their conclusions to the class.

Reading

1 Ask students to read the first two sentences of the article. Discuss the ways in which they are or are not individualists. They can refer to their answers in *Start up*.

2 Ask students to read the article and answer the questions. The final question is a free question where students can discuss their opinions at class level.

○▄ 1 Generation Y MySpace Generation   2 baby boomers Generation X
Yuppies   3 They are all digital activities   4 They don't distinguish between the online and the real world   5 It helps them keep up to date
6 Students' own answers

➕ Additional activity
(all levels)
Ask students to write a title for each paragraph.

Possible answer
Generation Y; Baby boomers and Yuppies; What Generation Y does; MySpace generation; Generation Y and the Internet

✳ Tip
Top margin p.18
Ask students to work in pairs and read the acronyms. Do they know people who fit the profiles? Do they fit one of the profiles? Ask students to cover up the top margin and dictate the definitions to the students. They try to remember the acronym. Discuss the two definitions of *marketing* and ask students to choose the one they prefer.

➕ Grammar test
Go to p.76 Teacher's Resource Book.

3 Ask students to find the words in the article.

> **O━** **Para 1:** be addicted to, trendspotters **Para 2:** high earning **Para 3:** keep up with **Para 4:** distinction, multitask **Para 5:** word of mouth

4 Ask students to use the results of the discussions in *Start up* to help them write about their purchases. Suggest they choose three typical purchases and analyse them in a paragraph each.

Vocabulary
Acronyms

Ask students to read the advice and answer these questions:
What are acronyms? When should they not be used? When may students come across them?
Then get them to match the abbreviations with their meanings.

> **O━** 1 g   2 c   3 f   4 h   5 b   6 e   7 a   8 d

Language spot
Present Perfect Simple or Continuous

Ask students to read the rules. Go through the Grammar reference with the students or set for homework.

Ask students to find examples of both tenses in the *Talking about my Generation* article and match the examples to the rules.

> **O━** trendspotters have been studying your generation's habits 4
> they have given it a name 1
> Marketers have been identifying groups of people for a long time 4
> What have you been doing this afternoon? 5
> I've been doing a quiz online. 5
> I've been writing to classmates. 5
> I've been downloading music. 5
> I've been watching my favourite soap. 5
> ...which experts have recently called the MySpace generation 1

1 Ask students to read the report and complete it with the words.

> **O━** 1 been   2 arranging   3 done   4 typing   5 printed
> 6 written   7 surfing   8 working   9 listening

2 In pairs, students discuss what they have been doing / have done that morning, inventing an office situation.

Reading

1 In pairs students choose a famous brand and imagine they are the company that made it. They then answer the questions in the top margin.

2 Ask students to read the article. At class level get students to tell you about the 4 Ps until you are sure that everyone understands. Then get students to summarise each one, in pairs if they prefer.

➕ Additional activity

(all levels)
Get students to write a short report based on their discussion in exercise 4.

➕ Photocopiable activity
Consumer profiles

Go to p.77 Teacher's Resource Book.

✳ Tip

Top margin p.20
Read the quotes in the top margin and ask students: *Do you have loyalty to particular shops or supermarkets? Do you respond to special offers in supermarkets or shops?*

✳ Tip

Dictate the definitions to the students, and get them to find the words in *Company profile*.
special offer a lower price available for a short period of time
discount card a card which gives customers a lower price
market share the percentage of sales a company has compared to its competitors

➕ Additional activity

(stronger students)
Ask students to find the words and expressions which mean:
1 a store that sells food, drink and household products (grocery store)
2 designed for customers with a high income, expensive and high quality (upmarket)
3 designed for customers with a low income, cheap and lower quality (downmarket)
4 food and other goods used in the home (groceries)
5 products that a shop sells with its own name on them (own-brand)

➕ Additional activity

(all levels)
Company profile, exercise 3, can become a project with students working in groups. Students should aim to answer the same sort of questions as in *Company profile*. They can put their projects on the wall when they have finished.

O─ Price: You may choose a high price for a high quality product with the right features. You may choose a low price if you are entering the market or you are a big store.

Promotion: You may sell your product face to face, with advertising or by targeting customer groups.

Place: You must get your product to your customers through effective distribution or direct selling.

3 Get students to match the verbs with the words and phrases.

O─ 1 d   2 e   3 a   4 c   5 b

4 Ask students in pairs to think about a product they have with them, for example, *pen*, *rucksack*, *trainers*, *mobile phone*, *watch*, *snack*. Get students to analyse how it has been marketed in relation to the 4 Ps.

5 In groups ask students to brainstorm until they agree on an advertising campaign. You can record commercials from the television, and / or take in some recent magazines and newspapers to help students choose. Students discuss the questions and make notes. Ask them to write a short presentation. Get groups to do their presentations to the class.

Company profile
Tesco

1 In pairs, get students to discuss the question. Round up at class level.

2 Ask students to read about Tesco and match the questions and answers.

O─ 1 E   2 C   3 D   4 A   5 B   6 F   7 G

3 Brainstorm the main supermarkets and ask students to choose one to research.

Meeting room
Opinions

1 In pairs get students to discuss what they think is happening in the picture. Play the recording and ask students to answer the questions.

O─ Laura proposes that the magazine should go online. Jamie disagrees with her.

2 Pre teach: *subscribe*, *loyalty*, *outsource*, *freelance*. Play the recording and ask students to make a note of the arguments for and against. Write up answers on the board so all students have all the answers.

O─ **For:** it will be like a club; it will bring more customers; online readers will be able to subscribe to the magazine; it will increase the loyalty of the readers; it will be interactive and have links; it will have a chat room; we will outsource the work
Against: it's not the right time; it won't be cheap; it will be a lot of work

Additional activity

(all levels)

Play the recording again and ask students to put the expressions in the order they hear them.

Additional activity

(weaker students)

Ask students to report back to the class if / where they had difficulties in the role play. Help them deal with the problems with remedial work, listening to the models again, going through the *Expressions* again, etc. It may be useful to ask students to repeat the activity later on in the course, where they will be able to see the progress they have made.

Additional activity

(all levels)

Photocopy the model answer and go through it with the students before they do the activity.

Writing bank
Reports 1 – Planning and writing
Go to p.54 Student's Book

3 Play the whole recording from exercise 1 and 2. Ask students to make a note of who says which point.

> It seems to me that ... L   I personally feel that ... L   I'm convinced that ... Y
> I'm positive that ... L   Yes, but don't forget ... Y   I would agree with that,
> but ... L   That may be true, but ... J   Even so ... J

Speaking

In pairs students are going to role play agreeing and disagreeing in a meeting. First get students to decide on the sort of company they work for. Then get them to read through the proposals and think of arguments in favour of their own proposals and against their partner's. Then they can do the role play. After a short time interrupt and ask some strong pairs to perform their role play, giving them feedback where necessary. Then ask all the pairs to continue.

Business know-how

1 Ask students to work in pairs and discuss the question.

2 Ask students to read the tips. In groups get students to discuss the tips in relation to their own behaviour and feelings. This is an ideal opportunity for students to continue using the *Expressions* list from the *Speaking* activity.

Writing

At class level go through the task with the students. Get students to suggest ideas for how the school could be marketed better. Give students the following expressions to use in their suggestions: *I feel / think / believe / I'm convinced / It seems to me that ...; I think it would be a good idea if ... ; Firstly ...; Secondly ...* etc.

Ask students to work in pairs and make notes for the list.

> **Possible answer**
> *Description*
> A new medium-sized language school – 180 students and 10 teachers. Five classrooms and a multimedia laboratory. Neighbourhood has residential areas, shops, bars and restaurants. Good public transport, parking nearby.
> *Competition*
> Two other schools: one has a good reputation, but is out-of-town and difficult to reach; the other doesn't have a good reputation.
> *USPs*
> Teachers with up-to-date qualifications; good classrooms and equipment; good exam pass rate; specializes in business teaching; good location.
> *Objective*
> We aim to attract 50 new students.
> *Promotional ideas*
> I feel that we should focus on how easy school is to reach, and it would be a good idea to point out the good exam results and its business specialization. Firstly we can advertise in local magazines and websites. Secondly we could offer free books to the first five students to enrol.

4 Leadership

Background

The qualities of a good leader are important to everyone in a business, and not just the people at the top. Due to the hierarchical nature of company organization, most people will be in a position of superiority to someone else in the chain of command. The qualities of a good leader will be of immediate relevance to them. But they will also be of importance to the employees they manage. And all employees are affected by the qualities, good or bad, of their managers.

Many business gurus, business schools, and management consultancies spend a lot of time and energy focusing on the qualities needed for effective leadership. Online research quickly reveals that there is no agreement on just how many qualities go to the making of a good leader. Some writers identify seven characteristics, some eight, and others as many as twenty. While some of these qualities could be considered innate, most of them can definitely be learned. And leaders or not, we all share some of those qualities already. So although we all can't or don't want to be leaders, we can still benefit by developing some core leadership qualities.

Some of these qualities are:

- **Good communication skills** If leaders aren't good communicators, they will never be able effectively to motivate their staff and develop good working relationships.
- **Vision** This is the ability to look beyond immediate concerns and focus on where the company, or department, should be in the future.
- **Emotional Intelligence** They need to have good Emotional Intelligence (EI) in order to understand and motivate their staff.
- **Motivation** Good leaders must also be able to understand what motivates people. This can include simple things like praise (telling people they have done well), appreciation (saying 'thank you') and recognition (openly crediting an achievement).
- **Integrity** Most commentators identify honesty and trustworthiness as an essential trait in any successful manager.
- **Commitment** This is both a commitment to excellence, but also to getting things done. Leaders need to be able to prioritize and do what they say they will.
- **Delegation** Good leaders delegate and empower others. They make it possible for others to take on more responsibility.
- **Humour and warmth** These are effective in most situations – leadership or not!

Additional activity

(all levels)
Ask students to write a paragraph about a leader they admire, giving reasons.

* Tip

Adjectives

formed from verbs
inspire – inspiring
persuade – persuasive
care – caring

formed from nouns
knowledge – knowledgeable

Start up

Look at the photos with the students and discuss in what way they illustrate leadership. Ask students to tell you the names of as many leaders (political, business, sport, etc.) as they can think of. Then get students to discuss these questions: *Are leaders necessary? What responsibilities do they have? What makes a good leader? Are leaders born or can they learn to be leaders?* Round up at class level.

Ask students to work in pairs and decide on a famous leader. Ask them to choose some qualities to describe him or her and some which he or she doesn't have.

Listening

1 Go through the table with the students. Then play the recording and ask them to complete the table.

My first boss	Cristina	Marek	Jodie
My job		Human Resources in an insurance company	language teacher
My boss's good points	calm, positive, enthusiastic, patient, good listener	competent	funny, inspiring, imaginative, enthusiastic, created a great atmosphere
My boss's bad points	expected you to work through your lunch break; difficult to have a life outside work	made people feel stressed; always in a panic; no sense of humour; not a good communicator	

2 Play the recording again and ask students to make notes of what the people learnt.

Cristina treat your customers and staff well, listen to them
Marek be a good communicator, be calm
Jodie create a positive atmosphere, if your staff enjoy their work then you can deal with their problems

Reading

1 Ask students to guess how the sentences could be completed before they read. Then get them to find the answers in the article.

Good leaders ...
work as a part of the team
encourage all their staff to work towards the same goal
ask their employees' opinions
give their staff freedom to make their own decisions
praise people's achievements
develop staff so they do their jobs better than their managers
identify the potential of others

2 Ask students to discuss the questions in pairs and then at class level.

3 Ask students to choose the six most important qualities for a leader.

Reading

1 Explain the situations to the students, possibly with stories from your own life. Then get them to discuss the questions in pairs.

2 Ask students to read the title of the article. What do they think it is going to be about? Ask students to read the article and answer the questions.

bullies criticize, ignore you, make you feel small, threaten or offend, make you look incompetent or feel a failure, change goals, and exclude people
bullying reduces company profits, there is more absenteeism and there are more resignations
get support, keep a written record, confront the person

3 Ask students to read the article again and discuss the questions at class level.

* Tip

When you are describing what qualities / skills are necessary for a job you often use these verb forms:
need to
They **need to** have emotional intelligence.
must be
They **must be** enthusiastic.
They **must be** able to take risks.
have to
Good leaders **have to** be trustworthy.
Leaders **have to** develop their staff.

➕ Additional activity

(weaker students)
Ask students to read the article on p.23 again and find:
● adjectives describing leaders.
● ways of completing these expressions:
good at ...
be able to ...

➕ Additional activity

(stronger students)
Students think again about the leader they discussed in *Start up*. Ask them to discuss in what ways that leader has the qualities and skills in the article on p.23.

* Tip

Top margin p.24
Ask students to discuss the quotes and decide which one they like best.

➕ Additional activity

(weaker students)

If students are having trouble with these modals, help them see how they are related to previous modals they have studied:

must go / have to go	*had to go*
don't have to go	*didn't have to go*
will go	*will have to go*
won't go	*won't have to go*
should go	*should have gone*
shouldn't go	*shouldn't have gone*

➕ Grammar test

Go to p.78 Teacher's Resource Book.

✱ Tip

Top margin p.26

Ask students to cover the top margin and dictate it to them. Then ask them if they know any recruitment agencies in their town / city.

➕ Additional activity

(all levels)

An alternative method for *It's my job:* Ask students to read the first three parts of the article and answer the first three questions. Then get the class to brainstorm what they think Sasha's daily tasks would be. Make notes on the board. Then get them to read the rest of the text and answer the last question. How well did their guesses match Sasha's jobs?

➕ Photocopiable activity

Keep talking

Go to p.79 Teacher's Resource Book.

Language spot

should have, had to, didn't have to, will have to

Ask students to complete the rules.

> **1** will have to **2** should have **3** had to **4** didn't have to

1 Ask students to read the case studies and complete them,

> **1** call **2** contacted **3** leave **4** find **5** change **6** lost

2 Get students to discuss the situations in pairs. Encourage them to use the language in *Language spot*.

3 Ask students to make notes of their ideas and exchange them in pairs.

It's my job

1 Pre-teach: *job seekers, self-motivated, networking*. Get students to discuss recruitment strategies in pairs.

2 Ask them to read the article and answer the questions. Discuss with the class if they would like to work in recruitment.

> **1** They help companies find the right person for jobs.
> **2** Sasha specializes in IT recruitment.
> **3** Sasha needs to be a good sales person, self-motivated, a good time manager. You need drive, communication skills and to inspire trust.
> **4** spend time on the phone, talking to job seekers and employers, visit companies, have face-to-face interviews with clients, do administrative work.

Small talk

Thinking time

1 Go through the questions. Play the recording and ask students to answer them.

> **1** Both Karen and Daniel went to the cinema and saw the same film.
> **2** Daniel liked the film more than Karen.
> **3** Karen feels embarrassed because she didn't want to disagree with Daniel, because she likes him.

2 Play the recording again and ask students to mark when they hear extra words or sounds. Then ask students to listen again and tell you what words she uses.

Oh no! Not at all. I was just / (erm) talking to a colleague.
How was my weekend? It was / (sort of) OK.
I went to the cinema on Saturday / (you know) with some friends.
/ (Well) I like Johnny Depp normally. / (I mean) He's an interesting actor, but it depends on the film. This one was a bit / (erm) strange.
Oh, / (well) so did I. I liked it, too.

3 Play the recording again and get students to number the expressions in the order they hear them.

1 er / erm   2 I'm sorry?   3 How was my weekend?   4 sort of
5 you know   6 Well …   7 I mean

Speaking

Go through the *Expressions* list again. Divide the class into pairs. Tell students to read their role cards and then hold conversations. After the first activity interrupt the students and remind them to use the strategies from *Expressions*.

Business know-how

Point out that one doesn't have to be a leader or manager to be successful in one's career. Get students to do the quiz individually. It reflects some of the qualities leaders have, and ranges from people skills to personal skills and individual preferences. Get students to score their answers and then compare the results in pairs. At class level discuss why each of the questions reflects leadership potential.

Writing

Ask students to read the extract from the email and answer these questions. *What are the problems Jackie has with her new manager? What does Jackie like about her? What was Jackie's old manager like? Who do you think is the better manager?*

Ask students to write an email back to Jackie giving her some advice. Encourage them to use the *Expressions* list from *Small talk*.

Possible answer
Hi Jackie
Your boss doesn't sound so bad. Maybe she feels that you are comparing her to your previous boss. Why don't you suggest that you all go out for a drink after work and get to know her better? You may find out that she is more human than you think! It would be a good idea to find out about the lists and systems that she likes to keep – it may help you enjoy your job more and get a sense of achievement. Good luck!

Additional activity
(all levels)
Students can repeat the *Speaking* activity with new partners to make it more challenging.
Alternatively they can choose new topics to discuss, e.g. a hobby or interest, a favourite festival, an interesting TV programme they saw.

* Tip
Leaders need a range of skills. These include:
- being good at completing tasks and wanting to move on to the next challenge
- being someone people turn to for help
- being able to express yourself clearly and tell people what you think of their behaviour
- being unafraid of public speaking
- actively like helping other people do their jobs well
- being able to focus on many things at the same time
- being someone who wants to find solutions to all sorts of problems
- being a quick thinker
- being able to show that you are calm when inside you may feel afraid or angry

Writing bank
Notices – News about staff
Go to p.52 Student's Book

5 Changing world

Background

Digital technology has transformed our lives at home and at work. In our free time we use the Internet to communicate with each other, to download and upload our own entertainment, to buy products and services. We book plane tickets, check museum opening times, keep up with the news, check the definitions of words, and send photos to friends.

These new patterns of online behaviour are having an enormous impact on the retail business. In the UK it is estimated that online spending is growing ten times faster than spending in shops. Although online spending still represents a small percentage of overall retail sales, the balance of spending is changing fast. And while we are busy downloading music and films, major music and media companies are struggling to maintain their profit margins and high street stores are cutting the prices of their back catalogue of CDs and DVDs. In the UK, downloads are now included in the official 'singles' charts. Meanwhile, digital cameras have overtaken the sale of film cameras, challenging the existence of the high street film developer.

The impact of digital technology on the workplace has been profound. It took less than a decade for emails to revolutionize business communications. However, instant communication can also have its downside. The average office worker now spends two to four hours every day dealing with emails. She or he receives around 65 emails and sends 20. About 25% of these incoming emails are external spam or internal 'noise' that can be deleted immediately.

So how will the new technologies affect our working lives in the future? In order to speed up production and services, and to reach new customers in foreign time zones, an increasing number of companies are operating 24 hours a day, seven days a week. Whereas 'shift workers' used to be assembly-line workers, today they are as likely to be graduates. In the USA, around 24 million people already work in a 24/7 culture.

Offices will have fewer individual enclosed 'offices' and more shared work spaces, where people simply plug in their laptops wherever they choose. At the same time, employees will become less office-bound. In 2006, 24 million Americans 'teleworked', working from home a part of the week. It is predicted that in the next few years more than half of US employees will spend at least two days a week out of the office.

Start up

Ask students to work in groups to discuss the questions about the future. Round up at class level.

➕ Additional activity

(stronger students)
Get students to think of examples of dotcom businesses they know and use. Ask them these questions:
● *Have you ever bought and sold on the Internet?*
● *Have you ever experienced spam mail, phishing or spyware?*

Vocabulary

Digital world

Ask students to match the words and definitions. Go through the answers and explain anything they don't understand.

Oꟙ 1 c   2 a   3 b   4 e   5 d   6 h   7 j   8 i   9 f   10 g

Language spot

will, be going to, will have to, will be able to, infinitive

Ask students to read the rules and match the sentences with the rules. Go through the Grammar reference with the students or set as homework.

➕ Additional activity

(all levels)

Get students to work in groups to brainstorm their ideas for exercise 1 before they write their sentences. Ask them to discuss the grammar they would use for each prediction.

✳ Tip

.com

The top level domain you can have for an internet site. It was established in 1985. Many countries have a **second level** domain:

- UK (.co.uk)
- Japan (.co.jp)
- People's Republic of China (.com.cn)
- Brazil (.co.br)

Other top level domains are: .biz .edu .gov .info .net .org

dotcom bubble between 1997 and 2001 many companies started on the Internet and were invested in, but went bankrupt because they didn't grow as fast as expected

➕ Grammar test

Go to p.80 Teacher's Resource Book.

✳ Tip

Top margin p.30

Discuss the quotes with the students. Ask them to translate them into their own language so they have the same humorous tone.

➕ Additional activity

(stronger students)

Students can do a class survey of camera use and write a short illustrated report.

➕ Additional activity

(weaker students)

Ask students to read the article again and answer the questions.

1 *When did Kodak start making cameras?*
2 *When did they make a strategic mistake?*
3 *How many jobs were lost at Kodak in 2006?*
4 *Have you ever seen a moblog?*
5 *What may only last 10 or 15 years?*
6 *What happened in the BBC in the 1980s?*

➕ Photocopiable activity

Contemporary trends

Go to p.81 Teacher's Resource Book.

> **○┭** 1 Sales are down 35%. We are going to go bankrupt.
> 2 Business people will have to do less travelling.
> 3 Business people will be able to work from home on the Intranet.

1 Ask students to write their own predictions for the future using *will* or *going to*. They can compare their ideas in pairs.

2 Ask students to complete the opinions with the expressions. Get them to discuss their answers in pairs. Discuss what students think of the predictions at class level.

> **○┭** 2 will face 3 will make 4 will have to do 5 won't go
> 6 are going to have to meet 7 won't be 8 will have to migrate
> 9 will cause 10 will download 11 will read 12 will have
> 13 will have 14 will work

Reading

1 Get students to discuss the questions in pairs.

2 Read through the factual predictions with the students and get them to discuss what will happen to the camera manufacturing business.

> **○┭** **Possible answers**
> The price of digital cameras will go down; camera technology will continue to improve; new companies will provide data storage, easy printing services etc. will develop; people will stop using film cameras at all.

3 Get students to work in groups of three or four. Read through the situation with the students. Ask one student to make a note of the decisions the group makes. Get the groups to present their ideas to the class and make notes on the board of the best ideas.

4 Pre-teach: *store, struggle, spread, losses, adapt, evidence, fade*. Ask students to read the paragraph headings and predict what the article will be about. What do they think Kodak's mistake and solution are? What could the digital trends and problems be?

Get students to read the article and discuss the questions back in their groups.

5 Ask students to read the article again and answer the questions.

> **○┭** 1 Professional photographers and the older generation; Students' own answers
> 2 You can store digital photos on a computer, or online in virtual space.
> 3 Because it was making heavy losses as it didn't start manufacturing digital cameras in the early 2000s.
> 4 Because the price of digital cameras fell, poorer countries have also started using digital cameras.
> 5 Printing shops have had to adapt, people make moblogs, Chinese law courts accept mobile phone photo evidence, Indian fishermen send photos of their catches to restaurants.
> 6 Because CDs with photos on may not last, programs and software changes so we may not have a permanent photographic record.

➕ Additional activity
Students can use the *Project* to make a short presentation to the class. Ideally they should use a computer and beamer to show the class the website in action.

✳ Tip

Top margin p.32
Ask students what they associate with the word *Google*. Go through the list and discuss the facts with the students. Which one do they find the most interesting / surprising?

➕ Additional activity

(all levels)
Ask students to read the *Company profile* again. Then ask them to cover the article and ask them these questions, If they answer in groups, the group which answers first gets a point.
Alternatively for weaker students dictate these questions and get them to answer them.
1 *How many languages does Google offer results in?*
2 *Who are its founders?*
3 *When did they meet?*
4 *How many employees did they start with?*
5 *What is 20% time?*
6 *How many staff does Google employ?*

✳ Tip

Skills needed in a search engine company
artificial intelligence making computers copy intelligent human behaviour
system design designing the set of programs that controls the way a computer works and runs other programs
networking a number of computers that are connected together so that information can be shared
security the activities involved in protecting data and computers from illegal use, viruses, etc.
data compression reducing data so it takes up less room

Project

In pairs students choose an area to research. They then go online and find two major companies selling the product or service. They need to try out the website and make notes on the areas in the list. They then need to discuss their overall feelings about the site as a conclusion. Students then write a review of the two sites comparing them, using the list as a guideline.

Company profile
Google

1 In pairs, get students to discuss the question.

2 Get students to find the numbers in the text and work out what they represent before they read it in detail. Then ask them to read and check their information.

> ⚷ 8 billion: the number of web pages Google provides access to
> 380 million: the number of users worldwide per month
> 150,000: the approximate number of advertisers on Google
> 370 million: its net income in dollars in 2005
> 2.5 billion: the number of search queries per day
> 2,000: the search queries answered per second between 6.00 am and noon

3 Discuss the question at class level. Ask students if they would like to work for Google and why / why not.

Meeting room
Adding and contrasting information

1 Remind students that the people work on a business magazine. Go through the stories that the editors are going to discuss so students understand them. Tell them that the meeting is to choose the story that will go on the cover. Play the recording and get students to answer the questions. Get students to write the names *Laura*, *Kim* and *Michael* in their notebooks so they can make notes.

> ⚷ 1 Laura: The top 10 businesses to invest in; Kim: The future of the Internet; Michael: China
> 2 The future of the Internet

2 Ask students to create a table with *for* and *against* at the top and the four stories down the left hand column. Play the recording and get students to make notes of the points.

⚷	For	Against
China	It's really interesting.	
	It compares the Chinese economy with the US.	We had an article on the Far East two issues ago.
Top 10 businesses	It's an important issue. It's a well-written article. There are surprising companies in the list.	It doesn't have the impact of some of the other topics. We want to appeal to the greatest number of readers.

25 trends	It's an interesting list.	I don't think it's strong enough for the front cover.
The future of the Internet	It's a great topic. It's really interesting.	
	There are amazing ideas.	
	Using the Internet affects all our readers.	
	They're going to be interested in it.	

3 Go through the *Expressions* list and then play the recording and get students to number the expressions in the order they hear them.

> **O—** 1 What's more 2 Mind you 3 However 4 And besides
> 5 Plus the fact that 6 All the same 7 I just wanted to add that

Speaking

Go through the *Expressions* list with the students. Ask them to repeat the sentences after you, paying attention to pronunciation and intonation.

In pairs get students to prepare the role play by reading their role card and thinking of other ideas. Then ask them to discuss the topic with their partners. After a short time interrupt and ask a strong pair to perform the role play, helping them where necessary. Then ask the pairs to perform the role play.

Business know-how

Ask students, in pairs to discuss which search engine they use, why and how they use it. Do they always get the results they want? Then get students to read the tips and discuss them with their partner, deciding which ones are new.

Writing

1 Ask students to read the emails and find the expressions.

> **O—** 1 Is there any chance of having...?
> 2 Let me know if....
> 3 I'm afraid...
> 4 But could we....

2 Go through the situation with the students and get them to write the email. Then ask students to swap emails and write a reply in class or for homework. They should either agree to meet or explain why they can't and suggest an alternative time.

➕ Additional activity

Before doing exercise 1, ask students to read the emails and ask them these questions:
● Who do you think Nadia is in relation to Chris?
● What is Nadia suggesting?
● When is she free?
● What does Chris suggest?

➕ Writing bank
Emails 2 – formal and informal language
Go to p.57 Student's Book

6 Working abroad

Background

Working abroad, either as part of a gap year, internship or more permanent arrangement, can help young people's careers and offer valuable experience. One in six British graduates now takes a **gap year** after college or university. This break between education and full-time employment (or between school and university), allows them to travel, work and develop, and can help them put together a much more impressive CV.

Working in a foreign country can offer many benefits to young people at the start of their professional careers. It can help them:

- develop self-confidence, initiative and independence
- improve language skills
- raise intercultural awareness
- develop transferable skills
- gain new insights and a different perspective

It can also impress future employers and improve job prospects. Working abroad demonstrates that the candidate has:

- initiative and motivation
- the ability to communicate and work in a team with people from a wide range of backgrounds and cultures

Working abroad not only improves many of the competencies and soft skills that employers are looking for, but also provides graduates with specific personal examples to discuss at an interview. They will be able to talk about teamwork, leadership, initiative, problem-solving, motivation, negotiation, etc. And even if the gap year travellers haven't worked during their period abroad, then the skills required to manage on a budget, make travel arrangements, and survive in unfamiliar environments can still be positively presented in CVs and interviews.

Internships are short-term remunerated jobs. Offering a living wage and a real understanding of how a company works, they are good for the intern's CV – and for his / her self-esteem. They are very popular and are mainly offered by larger businesses, especially in the media, finance or banking. But whether abroad or closer to home, they represent an important stage in the development of any young professional.

Working abroad, whether in the short- or long-term, can help us to understand how people from different cultures see things differently. It can teach us to examine our own prejudices and to see how others perceive us, including any negative perceptions. Greater sensitivity and understanding will always increase the chance of a successful business relationship.

➕ Additional activity

(stronger students)
Ask students to think about how knowing how other cultures work could be important for these people:
a doctor
an internet website designer
a business person

Start up

1 Get students to look at the pictures and describe the people. Ask students to discuss the questions in groups and round up at class level.

2 Go through the question with the class and discuss the examples given. Then ask students to make notes of their ideas. Round up at class level.

Vocabulary

Personality adjectives

1 Ask students to tick the adjectives that other nationalities might use to describe them. Encourage students to think about what other countries think, not what they think.

2 In pairs get students to compare their answers. Then get them to choose adjectives which *they* think are appropriate for people in their own country.

✳ Tip

culture a shared system of attitudes, beliefs, values and behaviour
culture shock a negative reaction to living in a new culture
stereotype the fixed idea that people have of a type of person or a culture, that is probably not true
intercultural between cultures

➕ Additional activity

(all levels)
After the listening task ask students to write advice to a business person doing business in their country in relation to the five issues. This could be a presentation to the class or a project.

➕ Additional activity

(weaker students)
Ask students to read the Case Studies again and answer the questions.
Gary
Where is Gary from?
What were his duties?
What was he chosen to do?
Why was his English useful?
Sophie
How long did she work in the company?
What were her duties?
Why was she nervous?
What language did they speak in the Chinese company?
Marco
Is he still in the company?
What is his current project?
Why did he have Spanish classes?
What does he like best about the experience?

✳ Tip

Top margin p.36
Ask students to speculate about the reasons for the two facts, e.g.
(Britons are seeking new experiences, better opportunities, want to learn a language, experience another culture, want a warmer climate.)
Ask students to cover the top margin. Write the three words on the board, and dictate the definitions to the class. They can check their answers by looking at the top margin.

➕ Photocopiable activity

Go to p.83 Teacher's Resource Book.

3 Ask students to pair the adjectives.

�	humorous, serious	disorganized, organized	unpunctual, punctual
	tolerant, intolerant	introverted, extroverted	emotional, reserved
	rude, polite	arrogant, modest	unreliable, reliable
	hard-working, lazy	patient, impatient	

4 Ask students to write a description of their own personalities using the adjectives, providing an example of their behaviour for each one.

Listening

Go through the exercise with the students. Then play the recording and ask students to match them with the issues.

�   1 Story 5   2 Story 3   3 Story 2   4 Story 1   5 Story 4

Reading

1 Ask students to discuss the questions in pairs. Then round up at class level.

2 Get students to read the Case Studies and answer the questions.

�   1 Gary   2 Sophie   3 Gary   4 Marco   5 Gary and Marco   6 Sophie
     7 Marco   8 Sophie

3 Get students to read the Case Studies again and discuss the questions at class level.

Reading

1 Ask students to read the introduction to the article. Then get students to work in pairs and discuss the advice and information that they would give to someone thinking of working abroad. Round up at class level.

�   **Possible answers**
     1 Look on the Internet, network, use trade magazines and journals, etc.
     2 Study a relevant foreign language, get a recognized qualification, etc.
     3 Do research about the country before you go, find expatriate groups when you are there, etc.
     4 Find out which countries are best for your sector, choose a country where you speak the language, etc.
     5 Find out about accommodation, update your passport, get health insurance or get hold of necessary documents, etc.

✳ Tip

Giving written advice

Ask students to find examples of the following language in the article.
Think about ...
Don't forget ...
You can / need / should / may / will ...
(An elementary knowledge) will ...
Encourage them to use this language when they give advice, e.g. for the *Project*.

✚ Grammar test

Go to p.82 Teacher's Resource Book.

2 Pre-teach: *horizons, red tape, underestimate, volunteer.* Ask students to read the article and match the headings in exercise 1 with the paragraphs in the text.

> ⚷ 1 B   2 D   3 E   4 A   5 C

3 Get students to discuss the questions in groups and then round up at class level.

> ⚷ reasons: help your career, expand your horizons, impress employers, show you are motivated and self-reliant, get new insights and a new perspective
> Students' own answers

Language spot
must, can't, may, might, could

Get students to match the captions with the pictures.

> ⚷ 1 c   2 a   3 b

Ask students to read the rules and match the captions and the sentences with the rules.

> ⚷ 1 2   2 4   3 3   4 5   5 1   6 6

Go through the Grammar reference with the students or set as homework.

1 Get students to work in pairs and speculate about the possible answers to the problems. Then ask them to choose the ones they like best and write their answers.

> ⚷ **Possible answers**
> 1 It may be for me. / It may be urgent.   2 He might be angry. / He may be busy.   3 Your email may be disconnected. / You might have very little work at the moment.   4 He may have been promoted. / He may be in love.   5 It might be criticism. / It may be praise.

2 Get students to do the quiz in pairs. Go through the example and encourage them to use the target language in their discussions.

> ⚷ 1 c   2 b   3 a   4 b   5 a   6 c   7 b   8 a

✳ Tip

Useful websites: www.cyborlink.com; www.executiveplanet.com; www.culturesavvy.com

Project

In pairs get students to decide on a country and do research online about the cultural areas in the list. Encourage different pairs to work on different countries so they can share their findings with the class. Get them to use the areas as headings for their advice. Students could present their findings to the class in a presentation and then write some advice to someone doing business in that country.

✳ Tip

Top margin p.38
Ask students to read the information and ask these questions:
What are the top charity concerns in your class? Do a class survey. Do people in your country have a gap year? Would you like a gap year?

✳ Tip

water cooler
a device that cools and dispenses water

water cooler gossip
as the water cooler is where office workers gossip and exchange stories, this expression means the gossip that goes round a company

Small talk
Suggestions and objections

1 Ask students to look at the picture. *Who is at the water cooler? How does Karen feel? What is Tim like?* Play the recording and ask students to identify Karen's problem. Discuss with the class what advice they would give.

> **O━** Her colleague at the next desk makes a lot of noise and Karen can't concentrate.

2 Play the rest of the recording and get students to make notes of the suggestions that Daniel and Tim give.

> **O━** talk to Louise about the noise; talk to her manager; write her an email; talk to her other colleagues; buy some ear plugs

3 Play the recording again and get students to write the initials next to the *Expressions*.

> **O━** Have you thought about / of ...? D   Why don't you ...? D   What if you ...? T   You could always ... D   Yes, but ... K   That might be all right but ... K   It's a good idea but ... T   I'm not sure about that because ... D

Pronunciation
Reinforcing adverbs

Read the instructions with the students and look at the example sentence. Then play the sentences and stop after each one so students can repeat them.

Speaking

Go through the *Expressions* list with the class. Ask them to repeat them after you, focusing attention on pronunciation and intonation. You can use the recording to do this activity if you prefer.

Divide students into groups of three and allocate one student each to be A, B and C. Ask them to read through their problems carefully. Each student takes it in turns to tell the rest of the group their problem. The group then gives advice. Encourage the student with the problem to think of objections, and all students to use the *Expressions*.

Stop the activity after a short while and give the class some feedback on the activity, then ask them to carry on. You can ask some stronger groups to perform in front of the class.

➕ Additional activity

(stronger students)
Students can write their own problems and work in new groups to continue the *Speaking* activity.

It's my job

1 Get students to work in pairs and discuss the question.

2 Ask students to read *It's my job* and answer the questions.

➕ Additional activity

(weaker students)

Get students to copy the questions out. Ask them to study the answers carefully for two minutes. Then ask them to cover their books and role play the interview.

✳ Tip

Students could make a poster where they 'pledge' to follow one of the tips. Then after a few weeks you can check to see how useful the students are finding the advice.

➕ Writing bank
CV1

Go to p.63 Student's Book.

🔑 1 She's got an internship in a charity.
2 She wanted to see how a big international charity works and work abroad.
3 She goes to volunteer fairs and interviews volunteers, she does office work, is responsible for the database, processes application forms, writes emails, goes abroad and visits projects.
4 She has learnt that improving lives has a positive impact on the economy.

Business know-how

1 Get students to discuss the question and round up at class level.

2 Ask students to read the tips and tick the ones they do already. Ask them to choose two tips and try them out.

Writing

In pairs get students to look at the form and think about the information required. Ask students to imagine a job they would like to do and then get them to copy and complete the form for themselves.

7 Ethical trading

Background

Ethical trading means looking beyond purely economic objectives to consider the moral implications of business decision-making, and the impact business activity has on the world. This has become increasingly important in world trade with the corporate scandals at Enron and WorldCom and the rise of ethical brands such as Fairtrade and Product Red.

The implementation of socially responsible policies can not only aid the environment or people in poor and war-torn countries, but also benefit businesses themselves. Companies can:

- build sales as customers are increasingly basing their choices on ethical principles
- attract investment as investors interested in ethical issues grow in number
- increase public trust in the business
- maintain staff loyalty and motivation by offering opportunities for development, treating them fairly, and transparently
- save money, e.g. through recycling and energy conservation

Today's multinationals recognize that ethical business can translate into future profits. Unilever took over Ben and Jerry's ice cream, Cadbury Schweppes added Green and Black's chocolate to its portfolio, L'Oreal took over Body Shop. (The Body Shop had achieved global sales of £708m by 2005. The business was founded by Anita Roddick in 1976 with an investment of only £7,000.)

The ethical consumer market isn't made up of only food and toiletries. It also includes transport, tourism, fashion, banking and finance. 'Ethical consumers' choose socially responsible investments, buy environmentally-friendly goods, print on paper made from wood from sustainable forests, eat food which is organic or where the producer got a fair price (Fair Trade) and, most importantly, avoid companies that do not provide ethical products. It's a market that is growing year on year. In the UK alone in 2005 the ethical consumer market was worth around £29bn, an increase of 11% on the previous year. At the same time, consumer boycotts of companies accused of unethical trading caused £3.2bn in loss of sales.

✱ Tip

Actions consumers take, in order of frequency:
- recycle materials
- buy something to support local shops
- talk to friends and family about a company's behaviour
- recommend a company because of its responsible reputation
- choose a product because of a company's ethical behaviour
- avoid a product because of a company's behaviour
- buy primarily for ethical reasons
- look for information about a company's ethical behaviour
- feel guilty about an unethical purchase
- campaign about an environmental issue

Dictate this list of actions to your students and discuss how often people in the class have done these things in the past six months.

Start up

1 Pre-teach: *brand name, organic, recycling, exploit, developing world*. Get students to do the questionnaire individually.

2 In pairs get students to compare their answers. Discuss students' scores at class level.

Reading

Discuss with students where the following products are grown: coffee beans, bananas, tea, oranges and cocoa beans. Discuss what sort of conditions a lot of the farmers have.

⚷ Possible answers

coffee beans – more than 50 countries, topped by Brazil, Colombia, Indonesia, Vietnam; Mexico, Ethiopia, India, Guatemala

bananas – Brazil, Latin American countries, Uganda, India, Philippines, etc.

tea – more than 50 countries, including India, Sri Lanka, Africa, China, etc.

oranges – South and Central America, South East Asia, etc.

cocoa beans – Côte d'Ivoire, Ghana, Indonesia, Nigeria, Brazil, Cameroon, Ecuador, Malaysia, etc.

➕ Additional activity

(weaker students)

Ask students to read the article again and match these verbs with nouns and phrases.

promote help work invest edit

(promote fair standards; help organize farmers, the environment, the community; work with producers; invest in development; edit the paper)

➕ Grammar test

Go to p.84 Teacher's Resource Book.

✳ Tip

Top margin p.42

Before you read, ask students if they have heard of any of the companies and if they know anything about them.

Ask students to cover the top margin and dictate the facts. Then they can uncover the facts and check their answers.

➕ Photocopiable activity
Ethical consumers

Go to p.85 Teacher's Resource Book.

➕ Additional activity

(all levels)

After listening to the speakers ask students if any of their arguments have made them change their minds since their discussion in exercise 1.

1 Pre-teach: *labour, handicrafts, premium, tuberculosis, malaria*. Ask students to read the article and answer the questions.

> **⌗** 1 A movement that promotes fair standards for international labour.
> 2 It started in the 1960s with shops selling handicrafts made by poor producers, and the first Fairtrade label appeared in 1988. It helped coffee farmers. In 2002 the current Fairtrade mark was designed.
> 3 It helps organize farmers into co-operatives and helps improve workers' conditions. It pays producers a fair price and a special premium to invest in development.
> 4 Coffee, tea, fruit juice, bananas, chocolate, fruit and nuts.
> 5 Created by the rock star Bono and supported by some famous brands, a percentage of Product Red products goes to a fund to fight disease.

2 Get students to discuss the questions in pairs. Round up at class level.

Language spot
The Passive

Ask students to read the rules and add examples from the article. Go through the Grammar reference with the students or set as homework.

> **⌗** 1 Producers are paid a fair price for their goods ...
> 2 ... handicrafts which were made by poor producers.
> 3 A new Fairtrade global brand was launched...
> 4 Special products with the Product Red logo have been created.
> 5 And more and more Fairtrade products will be bought every year.

Listening

1 Ask students to discuss the question in pairs. Round up at class level.

2 Go through the exercise with the students. Look at the pictures of the people and ask students to speculate. Then play the recording and ask them to match the people with the summaries.

> **⌗** 1 B   2 D   3 A   4 C   5 E

3 Play the recording again and get students to make notes of the examples the speakers give.

> **⌗** 1 Big businesses advertise sweets and sweet foods to children.
> 2 Many businesses try to make a positive impact on the environment.
> 3 Bill Gates and his charities.
> 4 Buy Fairtrade food and drink, organic clothes; choose transport that's less polluting; ethical companies selling computers and phones try to limit the damage they do and recycle more.
> 5 In India, big drinks manufacturers are polluting the water supplies; lots of the ingredients used by industry are destroying habitats such as the rainforest.

Vocabulary

Finance

Ask students to find definitions for the words in their dictionaries.

> **fraud:** cheating someone to get money, etc. illegally
> **bankrupt:** having no money, unable to pay your debts
> **conspiracy:** a secret plan by a group of people to do something illegal
> **shareholder:** an owner of shares in a company
> **assets:** something of value that a company or person owns
> **liabilities:** money owed by a company
> **stock:** portion of a company's capital owned by an investor
> **falsify:** alter a document, accounts, etc. illegally

Reading

Ask students to discuss in pairs if it is acceptable to: *say you are ill when you aren't; take home pens, notepads, etc. from your workplace, school; lie about where you are on your mobile phone; copy material off the Internet and call it your own; pocket change given to you by mistake by a cashier.* Round up at class level, avoiding making judgements about students' opinions.

1 Pre-teach: *to claim* (make an application for money; assert), *scandal, to sell off, trouble, illegally, to cover up, dairy.* Then ask students to read the article and do the exercise.

> **1** T **2** F **3** F **4** F **5** T **6** T

2 Ask students to read the article and the information in the top margin again and make notes.

> **Enron**
> *Type of business:* energy
> *Where company was based:* America
> *No. of employees:* 21,000   *No. of countries it operated in:* 40
> *Notes about the fraud:* invented figures to fool investors, encouraged investors but sold own stock before bankruptcy, provided friends and families with money
> *Result of fraud:* investors lost money; company went bankrupt in 2001. CEOs convicted in 2006.
>
> **WorldCom**
> *Type of business:* telecommunications
> *Where company was based:* America
> *No. of employees:* 85,000   *No. of countries it operated in:* 65
> *Notes about the fraud:* inflated assets by $11 billion by 2003
> *Result of fraud:* investors lost money; company went bankrupt in 2003; CEO found guilty of fraud and conspiracy and sent to prison for 25 years.
>
> **Parmalat**
> *Type of business:* dairy and food
> *Where company was based:* Italy
> *No. of employees:* 34,000   *No. of countries it operated in:* 30
> *Notes about the fraud:* invented assets to cover liabilities, and falsified accounts over 15 years
> *Result of fraud:* went bankrupt in 2003. 135,000 Italian investors lost money; managers tried for fraud.

✚ Additional activity

(stronger students)
Read out the following ethical dilemmas to students and ask them to discuss them.
● Is it ever appropriate to try to get inside information about a rival company?
● A worker in a pharmaceutical company finds out there are problems with a $15 million drug development project. Should the company stop him going to the authorities with his concerns?

✚ Additional activity

(all levels)
Crime and punishment
Dictate the words and the definitions separately and ask students to match them.

to convict   sentence   to try   to steal theft   thief   trial   guilty   innocent

● the crime of stealing from a person or place (*theft*)
● the person who steals (*thief*)
● to take something without permission, illegally (*to steal*)
● to examine evidence in court and make a decision about a person (*to try*)
● a formal examination of evidence in court by a judge, and often a jury (*trial*)
● having done something illegal (*guilty*)
● not guilty of a crime (*innocent*)
● the punishment given by a court (*sentence*)
● to decide that someone is guilty of a crime in court (*to convict*)

3 Ask students to work in pairs and discuss their opinions. Round up at class level.

Project

1 Brainstorm a selection of multinationals which are meaningful to students on the board and make sure that pairs are researching different companies.

2 Encourage students to make notes from the Internet so they don't simply print out texts. Ask them to make notes about the three areas. They then write a report with the three headings. Students could make posters, or do presentations of their findings.

✱ Tip

Top margin p.44
Ask students to tell you what the product is in the photo.
Ask students to read the information after studying *Company profile*. Ask them to explain what Richard Reed and *Innocent* mean in the quotes. They can write paraphrases of each quote.

➕ Additional activity

Play the recording again and ask students: *Why does Laura believe it is important to get factual information correct?* (Because readers rely on the accuracy of the information so they must never publish factual errors.)

➕ Additional activity

(weaker students)
Before beginning work on *Company profile*, revise food and drink vocabulary with the students. Write the following food categories on the board and ask students to brainstorm words.
● Meat
● Fish
● Vegetables
● Fruit
● Drinks
● Basic foods (e.g. bread)
● Snacks
● Dishes and meals (e.g. dessert, risotto, sandwich, roast, etc.)

Meeting room
Giving reasons why

1 Look at the picture with the students and ask them to guess why Kim is going to see Laura. Go through the questions with the students. Then play the recording and answer the questions.

> **O⊸** 1 because Kim has had one or two problems recently
> 2 several articles have been late, there were mistakes in the articles

2 Play the recording again and get students to make notes.

> **O⊸** not her fault; the writers didn't deliver them on schedule; the articles were so badly written she had to check grammar, spelling, etc.; she didn't have time to check on all the facts

3 Go through the *Expressions* list and then play the recording and get students to number the expressions in the order they hear them.

> **O⊸** 1 I admit that   2 The reason why   3 That's why   4 I grant (you) that
> 5 It's true that   6 You're right

Speaking

Go through the *Expressions* list with the students. Ask them to repeat the sentences after you or after the recording. Ask students to read through one situation at a time and then role play the conversations one at a time. Interrupt the activity after students have done one or two role plays and give feedback. Get some stronger pairs to perform to the class.

Company profile
Innocent

Get students to discuss their eating habits in pairs. Ask them to answer these questions: *What do you eat and drink to stay healthy? How much fruit do you eat in a week? Do you manage to eat a healthy lunch?*

Get students to read the *Company profile* and match the questions and answers.

Additional activity

(all levels)

Dictate these questions and ask students to answer them about *Company profile* without reading it again.

1 Who founded *Innocent*?
2 When did they start?
3 How much did they spend at first?
4 Why did they have a 'Yes' and a 'No' bin?
5 What don't you find in *Innocent* drinks?
6 What is the name of their headquarters?
7 What do they do on Monday?
8 What was the company turnover in 2006?
9 How many drinks did they sell a week in 2006?
10 What sort of packaging do they use?
11 How do they transport their fruit?
12 What proportion of their profits goes to charity?

Writing bank

Emails 2 – Formal and informal language

Go to p.57 Student's Book.

1 E 2 B 3 G 4 F 5 A 6 C 7 D

Get students to plan an ethical company in groups making notes about the points in the list. Then ask them to present their ideas to the class.

Business know-how

1 Tell students what you do to help the environment. Then in pairs get students to discuss the question.

2 Ask students to read the tips and discuss the questions.

Writing

Ask students to read the email and answer the question: *Why is the boss asking for a meeting?* Then get students to write an answer to Raul, according to the instructions. They can write this in class or for homework.

8 Diversity

Background

Diversity is generally defined as acknowledging, accepting and valuing differences between people irrespective of age, gender, ethnicity, class, physical and mental ability, race, sexual orientation and religion. Management gurus and the business press have argued for some time that diversity in the workplace can make companies more profitable and help solve recruitment problems. Businesses which encourage diversity deliver better products, respond more quickly to the market place, and consequently make higher profits.

The four main reasons for companies to manage diversity are:

- to improve productivity and competitiveness
- to encourage better working relationships among employees
- to enhance social responsibility
- to fulfil legal requirements

Diversity issues are likely to become even more important in the future as the populations of countries become increasingly mixed. The worldwide economy and increasing globalization also demand more interaction from people of different cultures, beliefs and backgrounds. But in a highly competitive global economy, a diverse workforce can be the key to maintaining and increasing profits. The principal benefits to a business for encouraging diversity in the workplace include:

- increased productivity among all workers, especially among groups that have often been underused or discriminated against
- improved staff recruitment and retainment, with increased motivation and company loyalty
- increased flexibility with employees from different backgrounds bringing varied talents and experience
- increased creativity and innovation
- enhanced reputation

And all of the above will result in greater profitability.

Gender is an issue in terms of equality opportunities and discrimination. A recent EU report revealed that while women account for more than 50% of university-level students in nearly all member states, they earn 15% less than men as soon as they join the workforce. Forty percent of women work in education, health or public administration compared to 20% of men. Over 32% of working women are in part-time jobs compared to 7% of men. Within businesses, women hit the 'glass ceiling' and often fail to rise to top management jobs. This discrimination has economic consequences. A government-commissioned enquiry calculated that the UK economy was losing £23bn per year due to the wasting of women's talents.

✳ Tip

Encourage students to use expressions for agreeing and disagreeing.
What do you think?
Don't you agree?
Yes, absolutely.
You're absolutely right.
That's true.
I agree. / I disagree.
Yes, but don't you think ...
Yes, but, on the other hand ...
In my opinion ...
Actually, I think ...

➕ Photocopiable activity
Diversity and discrimination
Go to p.87 Teacher's Resource Book.

Start up

1 Ask students to look at the pictures in pairs and answer the questions. Round up at class level.

2 Ask students to decide on their reaction to each of the statements and then compare their answers with their partner.

3 At group and then class level discuss opinions and allow students to debate their opinions.

Reading

1 Ask students to look at the headline and discuss the meaning of the word 'Discrimination'. Then get them to read the article quickly and find out why each person has experienced discrimination. Round up at class level.

🔑 Andrew: being disabled; Carmen: being a woman; Hind: being Muslim; Leon: being overweight; Marta: being older than other applicants

➕ Additional activity

(all levels)

Discuss these questions with the students.

Should disability make a difference when people apply for jobs?

Should companies with fewer female managers than male managers do something about it?

Should it matter what people wear to work?

Should a person's physical appearance affect their job prospects?

Should age make a difference to getting a job?

➕ Additional activity

(stronger students)

Ask students to work in pairs and write sentences suggesting solutions to the problems below. Remind them to use conditionals in their sentences.

- *I have to be able to drive for my new job but I keep failing my driving test.*
- *My colleagues make fun of one of our secretaries because of her accent.*
- *I want to go for a job interview for a different company, but I don't have any holidays left.*

➕ Grammar test

Go to p.86 Teacher's Resource Book.

✳ Tip

Top margin p.48

Ask students to read the quote. *Where do they think they might read a quote like this?* (On a company's job application forms and in company policy documents, possibly on a company's website)

➕ Additional activity

(all levels)

Dictate these questions. Then play the recording again and ask students to answer them:

1. *What three things does research say organizations gain from diversity?*
2. *What will your company become if you encourage diversity?*
3. *When will your staff work better in teams and communicate better?*
4. *What is the final advice the presenter gives?*

2 Get students to read the article more carefully and answer the questions.

1. Because a recent study proves that 'normal' colleagues take more time off work.
2. Because she feels she is in a minority and is not included in the male networking groups.
3. Because she doesn't think how you dress should be an issue but how well you do the job.
4. He is well-qualified, gets on with people, and wants to work with people. He is overweight.
5. Because they think older candidates are less flexible, may cause problems, and may get paid more.

Language spot
Conditionals

Ask students to read the rules and then find examples of conditionals in the article.

If I went for a job interview, I wouldn't be able to convince the interviewers that I'm not a health risk.

But if I got this job, would I be treated the same as the men?

If I go for a job interview, I expect to be asked the usual questions.

Would you wear your head scarf if we gave you the job?

If you are the best candidate, you should get the job.

And if I looked different, I'd be able to get a good job.

If I went for a job interview, I might be able to make a good impression.

Perhaps if I lost weight, I could get a job.

Plus, if they employ an older person, they may have to pay a higher salary.

If I were younger, I wouldn't have a problem getting a job. It's not fair.

Ask students to complete the sentences in class or for homework.

1. were, would invest   2. accepts, won't have to / accepted, wouldn't have to   3. won, would quit   4. didn't spend, would be able to   5. help, will be able to / helped, would be able to   6. heat, boils   7. see, will tell

Listening

Ask students to think about why it is a good idea to encourage diversity in the workplace and how a company could introduce it. Then ask them to read the notes – do they have the same ideas? Then play the recording and get students to put the points in the order they hear them.

A 3   B 1   C 2   D 5   E 6   F 4

Vocabulary
Word-building

Ask students to make as many words as possible.

⊙━ employee   employed   unemployed   employment   unemployment
employable   employability
comfort   comfortable   uncomfortable
product   productive   unproductive   production   productivity
satisfaction   dissatisfaction   satisfy   satisfied
appropriate   inappropriate   appropriateness   appropriacy
inappropriateness
discriminate   indiscriminate   discriminated   discrimination

Reading

1 Ask students to work in pairs and discuss the statistics.

2 Ask the students to look at *Women in the workplace* and check their answers to exercise 1. Round up at class level.

⊙━ 1 F   2 T   3 F   4 T   5 T   6 T   7 T   8 F

3 In pairs get students to discuss the situation in their country, also comparing the information in the article.

Project

Get students to work in pairs and discuss the questions. Encourage them to come up with questions they would like the answer to for each area. Then get them to use the suggested sites for their research. The questions can be used as headings for their paragraphs.

Small talk
Correcting yourself

Ask students to look at the picture and discuss what might be happening and how Karen and Daniel feel.

1 Play the recording and ask students to answer the questions.

⊙━ 1 Sally is criticizing Gary's performance because he comes in late and leaves early.
2 That women have problems managing men.
3 Because she is angry with Daniel.

2 Play the recording and get students to answer the questions.

⊙━ 1 To apologize for calling him sexist.
2 He meant to say that some men don't like having women for bosses.

3 Play both the recordings and ask students to tick the expressions they hear.

⊙━ That isn't what I meant   what I meant was   what I'm saying is
I didn't mean to say

✳ Tip

Talking about statistics
on average
well below
more likely
fewer + *countable noun* than
the same
less / more + *noun* than
slightly less / more

✳ Tip

Top margin p.50
Ask students to look at the photo and read the quotes. *Why do you think the people don't like the experiences they describe?* Ask students to read the information and discuss the implication of this for employers. (Employers could lose valuable skilled staff by not having a policy that welcomes disabled people.)

✳ Tip

As this unit deals with disability and difference, teachers need to prepare for possible difficulties in the classroom, where they may have disabled students, or people of different ethnic origins. If appropriate, these students can talk about their experiences, but there must be an atmosphere of respect. If you cannot guarantee this, it is best to avoid personalization.

➕ Additional activity

(weaker students)

Ask students to read *It's my job* again and answer the questions.

1 *How do tactile pavements help Max?*
2 *How does Braille help Max?*
3 *How does the computer help Max?*
4 *What courses has he done?*
5 *What help did his colleagues have?*

✳ Tip

Politically correct (PC) terms

Language which avoids causing offence to social minorities. In the press 'PC' is often criticized for making people too self-conscious about what they can and can't say. However, in the diverse workplace, an awareness of appropriate terms helps workers avoid offence and encourages understanding.

- 'chairperson' or 'chair' not 'chairman'
- 'visually impaired' is often preferred to 'blind' and includes people who have a variety of eye problems
- 'deaf' is still acceptable, but deaf people don't like 'hearing impaired'
- 'hard of hearing' is OK for people with a variety of hearing difficulties
- 'woman' not 'lady' or 'girl'
- 'disabled' is preferred to 'handicapped', though the noun 'handicap' is acceptable
- 'black' is PC to describe someone of Afro-Caribbean origin but 'coloured' is considered offensive
- 'Asian' is PC to describe people originally from the Far East or the Indian subcontinent
- 'speech impairment' is preferable to 'stutter' or 'stammer'

➕ Writing bank

Letters 1 – Making payments

Go to p.58 Student's Book.

Pronunciation

Word stress

Play the recording and get students to underline the stressed words, then listen and repeat. Explain to students that we stress certain words when we speak to emphasize corrections (*I'm not meeting <u>Alan</u>, I'm meeting <u>Andrew</u>.*) or to emphasize what we mean (*It's the <u>men</u> that are the problem.*).

> 🔑 2 <u>Sandra's</u> a much better designer than <u>Tim</u>.
> 3 No, not <u>Tuesday</u>, <u>Thursday</u>.
> 4 She's going to arrive at <u>twelve</u>.
> 5 No, it <u>isn't</u> finished.
> 6 Well, it's <u>one</u> of the best.

Speaking

Go through the *Expressions* list with the students. Students are going to come out with extreme opinions and then moderate their sentences. Go through the example with the students and then ask them to have the conversations. Encourage them to exaggerate their responses so the student with the opinion has to moderate how they express their ideas.

It's my job

1 Ask students to discuss the question.

2 Get students to read *It's my job* and answer the questions.

> 🔑 1 training and development, dealing with younger people on work placements, running training courses, using the phone and computer, typing, giving presentations
> 2 tactile pavements, speaking lifts with Braille
> 3 special software on his computer, computer that tells him what he has written, printer that prints Braille

Business know-how

Go through the instructions with the students. Ask students to go through the advice in pairs and identify the most useful tips. Can students think of any other pieces of advice? Round up at class level.

Writing

Ask students to make notes on the approach of their school, workplace or a business, either through research on the Internet or by asking their school for documentation. They should write their viewpoint of these policies and suggest improvements based on their work in this unit. Get them to use their notes to write a paragraph. Suggest they use the verbs provided.

9 Brands and values

Background

A **brand** is the collection of features which distinguish a business, or one of its products, from the similar products or services of its competitors. These features include its name, slogan, logo, and packaging. In an increasingly crowded and competitive marketplace, it is vital for producers to establish **brand awareness** and to create **brand loyalty**.

Branding offers businesses clear benefits:

- it differentiates its products from its competitors'
- it promotes a distinctive image which represents the company's core values
- advertising encourages brand loyalty and goodwill from its customers
- brand loyalty allows the business to charge a premium price, possibly higher than those of its competitors
- a brand name makes it easier for the company to promote itself globally

With **brand extension**, an existing brand can be used to sell new products. The Virgin brand covers, for example, air and rail travel, retail, credit cards, mobile phones and the internet. A successful brand will embody the **core values** of a business. With Virgin, these include quality, excellent customer service, innovation, and a sense of fun.

Large companies also promote sports and arts events for several reasons. Among other things, **sponsorship** enables them to:

- gain a better return on their investment than conventional advertising. For the 2006 World Cup in Germany, 15 companies including Adidas, Coca-Cola and McDonald's paid £28m each in order to become official sponsors. Adidas has spent $80m to become the exclusive track shoes sponsor of the 2008 Beijing Summer Olympics.
- gain increased brand recognition in their target market. So banks and financial organizations often sponsor cultural events, while mobile phone and soft-drink companies sponsor musical events and the charts.
- adjust or reinforce their image. Sportswear manufacturers seek to associate themselves with qualities such as challenge and success, hence Nike sponsors Manchester United and Maria Sharapova.

Brands can be threatened by negative publicity and information (often spread by the Internet), cheaper no-brand goods, and the pirating of their products. The value of fake goods in Britain now tops £10bn.

➕ Additional activity

(weaker students)
Write these words on the board and then read out one definition at a time. Ask students to match the words with the definitions.

respectful   creative   progressive caring   dynamic   trustworthy passionate

having a lot of energy and enthusiasm (*dynamic*)
reliably honest and sincere (*trustworthy*)
modern and in favour of new ideas and change (*progressive*)
using imagination and creativity to invent new things (*creative*)
having strong positive feelings and emotions (*passionate*)
kind and helpful (*caring*)
showing respect for someone (*respectful*)

Start up

1 Get students to work in pairs and read the Business Factbox. Go through the core values list with the students. Then ask them to think of which values in the list could be the core values of their school. They can also think of others.

2 Ask students to work in groups and discuss the companies and their core values.

3 Tell the students that the core values come from the websites of the companies. Ask students to try and match the companies with the core values.

> ⚷ A Reebok   B Yahoo!   C Microsoft   D Coca-Cola
> E Body Shop   F British Airways

Reading

1 Ask students to think of the brands they associate with chocolate as an example, writing their answers on the board. Then get them to do the same for the other words individually.

* Tip

Ask students to form as many words as possible from the words in bold. They will find some help in the article.

brand branded unbranded branding
associate associated association
communicate communication communicator
compete competitive competition competitor
promote promotion promoter promotional

✚ Additional activity

(all levels)

Ask students to read the article again and answer these questions:

When is branding successful?
What are 'brand recognition' and 'brand equity'?
Why is packaging important?
What is special about the brand created by Coca-Cola or McDonald's?
What are the keys to writing a successful slogan?

✚ Additional activity

(stronger students)

Get students to choose a big brand company and research their sponsorship activities online.

* Tip

waffle maker A waffle maker is a machine for making waffles, (crisp, flat cakes with a pattern of squares on them, eaten hot with sweet sauce, cream, etc.)

✚ Grammar test

Go to p.88 of the Teacher's Resource Book.

2 In pairs get students to compare their ideas and think of words and images that they associate with the brands.

O🔑 **Possible answers**
sunglasses: Gucci, Diesel, Police, Ray-Ban, Byblos, Vogue
computers: Dell, Hewlett Packard, Compaq, Apple, IBM, Sony
coffee: Nescafe, Illy, Lavazza, Starbucks
perfume: Chanel, Yves Saint Laurent, Guerlain, Calvin Klein
batteries: Energizer, Duracell
mobile phones: Vodaphone, Nokia, Motorola, Sony Ericsson, Samsung
petrol: Shell, BP, Esso, Q8, Texaco
watches: Swatch, Rolex, Casio, Sekonda, Omega, Breitling, Tag Heuer
shampoo: Garnier, Pantene, L'Oreal, Clairol, Redken, Aveda, Dove

3 Go through the questions with the students and discuss the possible answers to them before they read. Then ask them to read the article and match the paragraphs with the questions.

O🔑 A 2   B 6   C 5   D 1   E 3   F 4

4 Get students to read the article again and discuss and answer the questions about a successful brand in their country.

Company profile
Nike, Inc

1 Ask students to discuss the questions. Round up at class level.

2 Pre-teach: *waffle maker, reigning champion.* Ask students to read *Company profile* and answer the questions.

O🔑 1 1964: Phil Knight and Bill Bowerman set up Blue Ribbon Sports; 1971: they established their brand identity with the 'Swoosh'; 1972: Launched their first line of Nike footwear; 1984: They launched the Air Jordan shoe; 2004: Its sponsored athletes won 50 gold medals and international sales exceeded sales in the US
2 It is the name of the Greek goddess of victory; Students' own answers

Language spot
Past Perfect

Ask students to complete the rules.

O🔑 1 Past Simple   2 Past Perfect

Ask students to read the article again and find examples of the Past Perfect.

O🔑 Phil Knight set up the business with Bill Bowerman, who had been his college athletics coach.
Bowerman had got the idea from his wife's waffle maker.
They had established their brand identity the previous year.
They had also named the brand Nike.
Nike's race to success had begun.

* Tip

Top margin p.69

Ask students to look at the picture. *What is the person doing? Do you like this sort of sport? What sort of people do this sort of sport?* Ask students to read the quote and answer the questions:
What are the X Games?
Do they have sponsors?
What do the fans think of the sponsorship?

➕ Additional activity

(weaker students)
After doing each listening task, play the recording again but let students follow it in the Listening scripts.

Ask students to brainstorm explanations for the situations using the Past Perfect. Then get them to write the best ideas in class or for homework.

> **O─┅ Possible answers**
> 2 She had studied / practised a lot. 3 They had had an argument.
> 4 The computer had broken down. 5 He had called the USA for work.
> 6 She had passed her driving test.

Listening

1 Ask students to look at the picture and discuss what is being sponsored and who the sponsors are. Then ask students to work in pairs and discuss the questions. Round up at class level and make notes on the board.

2 Play the recording and ask students to make notes of Cristina's answers to the questions in exercise 1.

> **O─┅ 1** almost any major event, from car racing to athletics; tours by pop artists; TV programmes; a car manufacturer will give money to a TV series to feature its vehicles; smaller companies support local athletics teams or charitable events or sponsor individual students through university
> **2** Adidas – the World Cup in Germany; Formula 1: Vodafone – McLaren Mercedes; Intel – BMW; Martini – Ferrari; American Express – the Rolling Stones in their 2006 World Tour
> **3** most advertisements are very direct, they're designed to sell a specific product; sponsorship aims to improve a company's image or brand awareness, links to certain qualities and values, its message is softer

3 Ask the question at class level. Then ask students to listen to the second part of the recording and put the reasons in the correct order.

> **O─┅** a 4 b 3 c 1 d 5 e 2

4 Get students to discuss the questions in groups. Remind them to use expressions of agreement and disagreement (p.7). Round up at class level.

Speaking

1 Ask students to look at the sponsors and the sponsorship opportunities and decide which sponsors would benefit from sponsoring which opportunity. Students should be able to justify their decisions.

2 Get each group to talk about one opportunity to the class and explain their reasons.

Meeting room

Explanations and reasons

1 Ask students to look at the picture and answer the questions.

2 Play the recording once and ask students what Yusuf is suggesting for the magazine. Go through the questions with the students and then play the recording. Get students to number the points in the order they hear them.

* Tip

Top margin p.70

Ask students: *Do you prefer Coca-Cola or Pepsi? Why? Do you think you could tell the difference if you were blindfolded?* Get them to read the top margin text and ask them what happened in the people's brains when they knew they were drinking Coca-Cola, and what happened when people didn't know which drink they were drinking.

➕ Additional activity
(all levels)

Play the recording again and ask students to summarize in their own words Yusuf's ideas.

✳ Tip

For the *Speaking* activity ask each student to brief the group on the situation in their own words. At that point they are all working for the same company and need to challenge the first students to explain and justify their decisions.

➕ Photocopiable activity
A new brand

Go to p.89 Teacher's Resource Book.

🔑 A 3   B 2   C 5   D 6   E 1   F 4

3 Play the recording again and get students to tick the expressions they hear.

🔑 Can you explain why …?   I don't understand why …
Although …   However, …   As a result …

Speaking

Go through the *Expressions* list with the students. Ask them to repeat the phrases after you, paying attention to pronunciation and intonation.

Divide the class into groups of three. First put As, Bs and Cs together so they can prepare reasons to justify their position. Each student should make notes of their reasons before joining their group. The groups then take turns to role play the situation.

Reading

Ask students to read the article and list the things a name should achieve for a brand.

🔑 A name has to create positive associations, be memorable, have emotional appeal, encourage sales, reflect a company's ethos and goals, communicate a product's qualities and USPs.

Project

1 In pairs students choose at least three names and decide what products they could be for.

2 Ask students to invent a new product and give it a name. To find a good name they can use dictionaries and online dictionaries, and thesauruses.

3 Students should prepare a talk divided into the four sections indicated in the questions. If possible they should prepare visuals and graphics.

Business know-how

Go through the instructions with the students and ask them to follow the instructions carefully. They only need to write notes at the moment.

➕ Writing bank
Emails 3 – Arranging a conference

Go to p.61 Student's Book

Writing

1 Ask students to read the Personal statement and compare the points with the notes they made.

2 Ask students to write their Personal statements using the model as a guide.

10 Office life

Background

Improved technology in the shape of wireless networking, fast Internet access and cost-saving software, is transforming the workspace and the way people work.

- **Voice over Internet Protocol** (VoIP) allows two or more callers to communicate via their computers.
- **Hot-desking** areas allow visitors, freelancers and permanent staff simply to plug in their laptops wherever they choose, cutting down the need for fixed work stations.
- An office-wide **wireless network** allows staff quickly and easily to exchange information while also clearing away a confusion of cables.
- **Video conferencing** cuts down the need for expensive and time-consuming travel.

These changes mean that employees can be much more flexible about where they work. They can now keep in close contact with the office on the road and from home. Teleworking allows employees to reduce commuting, work in their home environment, and enhance their lifestyle (and often their productivity). Improved technologies also mean that secretarial and IT services no longer have to be in-house, but can be outsourced to other suppliers.

Flexible working is leading to smaller, cheaper offices. It should also lead to a better work-life balance. However, the pressures of modern business life and 24/7 communications can damage your health. In Japan they call it *karoshi*. In China it's known as *guolaosi*. And what they mean is 'working yourself to death'. There is no specific word in English, but the long-hours' culture and its related stress levels are now a part of modern working life. A US survey confirms that long working hours increase an employee's chances of illness and injury. They can cause hypertension, fatigue, and even strokes and heart attacks. For this reason the EU seeks to limit working hours to a weekly maximum of 48. Average work hours in the UK are 43.6 per week, over 3 hours more than its European counterparts. What's more, 1 in 6 of the UK workforce are now working up to 60 hours per week. Interestingly, 65% of the UK workforce do not take the statutory 60-minute lunch break. The average break is now under half an hour and most employees choose to remain at their workstations. People simply cannot be separated from their PCs.

➕ Additional activity

(weaker students)
Make sure students can talk about Heidi and their own space by going through these adjectives.

The office
tidy – untidy / messy
cluttered – uncluttered
organized – disorganized
comfortable – uncomfortable

Start up

1 Ask students to read the introduction and answer the questions: *Whose is the office? What does she do? Is it tidy? Does she like it?* Get students to look at the photo and match the descriptions with the parts of the photos.

> 🔑 5 desk   2 chair   1 computer   8 mug   4 pictures
> 9 office essentials   6 plant   3 MP3 player   7 paper

2 Ask students to discuss what sort of person Heidi is, giving reasons for their opinions. Round up at class level.

3 In pairs get students to describe their work space. Ask them to explain how it reflects their character and interests.

Reading

1 Ask students to read the title of the article and guess what a Cube farm is. Get students to read the chat room and match the people with the preferences.

> 🔑 1 BCF   2 BCDF   3 AGH   4 EG

➕ Photocopiable activity
Work spaces
Go to p.91 Teacher's Resource Book.

2 Ask students to read the message board again and copy the table and make notes.

🔑 Open plan		Private office	
for	*against*	*for*	*against*
communicate more with your colleagues	distracting because people come and talk to colleagues	get more work done	isolated and lonely
			too quiet
ask questions without getting up from desk	you find out too much about your co-workers	use phone when you like, etc.	
productive if there are rules		people can pop in but you can be quiet	

3 In pairs get students to discuss their ideas about open plan and private offices. Round up at class level.

Project

Ask students to work in groups. Go through the instructions with the students. They must reach agreement about each decision. Ideally they should present their decisions to the whole class.

Language spot

must have, can't have, might / could have

Ask students to match the captions and the pictures. Then get them to complete the rules.

> 🔑 1 a   2 c   3 b
> might / could have   can't have   must have

Go through the rules with the students. Then go through the Grammar reference with students or set it for homework.

Get students to complete the sentences in class or for homework.

> 🔑 1 must have been   2 can't have understood / followed   3 must have passed   4 must have dropped / lost   5 must have gone out / stayed out   6 can't have arrived

Reading

1 Ask students to look at the reading and tell you what sort of publication it is. Get students to read the sentences and then scan the articles and match the sentences with the articles.

> 🔑 a 4   b 3   c 5   d 1   e 2

✳ Tip
Adjectives
distracting
messy
isolated
lonely
productive
quiet

✳ Tip
Top margin p.74
Ask students to discuss how Stelios's idea is different from how you usually rent offices.

➕ Additional activity
(stronger students)
Read out the following situations to the students. Ask them to work in pairs to prepare and then write the best explanations for each situation in class or for homework.
1 Ten members of the sales team resigned last year.
2 Jim is reading a letter about his job application. He looks very happy.
3 Markus is in a terrible mood today.
4 Carlos spent most of the morning on the phone.
5 Julia looks really suntanned and relaxed.

➕ Grammar test
Go to p.90 Teacher's Resource Book.

Additional activity

(weaker students)

Ask students to read the articles again and answer these questions.

How many Japanese have died of Karoshi? How many hours a week do Americans work on average? Why don't companies like blogs? How many sandwiches are eaten in the UK each day? How long is an average British lunch break? What happened in Spain in 2005? What do 55% of Americans do? How old is Polly? What happened to Polly at 1.00 am? How many graduates started with Polly? How many are there now?

Additional activity

(stronger students)

At class level ask students to compare facts from their own country with some of the facts in the articles. Brainstorm questions they would like to find out the answers to, e.g. *What is the average cost of lunch? Do people write work blogs? Do people overwork?* etc.

Get students to try and find out the information on the Internet or through other research. (They may not be able to find the answers, but that is also an interesting result.)

✳ Tip

Top margin p.76

Ask students what they know about internships: *Are they permanent? What are they for? Are they paid?* Ask them to read the definitions and check their answers. Pre-teach: *Anticipation, Disillusionment, Confrontation, Competence, Culmination.* Ask students to read the stages of internship and ask them if the stages are similar to other experiences, such as starting a new course.

✳ Tip

intern someone who works in a temporary position. The emphasis is on education. It can be either paid, unpaid or partially paid.
internships provide training, mentoring, work experience, networking experiences and a reference.

2 Get students to discuss the questions in pairs. Round up at class level.

> **Article 1:** When a worker dies from working very long hours. The USA has the longest working hours in the world. You can have accidents or become ill if you overwork. Students' own answers
> **Article 2:** Students' own answers
> **Article 3:** Students' own answers
> **Article 4:** She had a terrible work experience although it was a very well-paid job. She wrote a novel. Students' own answers
> **Article 5:** Students' own answers

Small talk
Surprising news

1 Ask students to look at the picture and describe Daniel's expression. Then get students to listen and make a note of Daniel's news.

> He's getting some new office furniture.

2 Ask students what *gossip* is: *Is it always true? What happens to a story when it is passed from person to person?* Play the recording and ask students to make a note of the names of the people speaking. Then play the recording again and ask students to make a note of the stories. Ask them what has happened to Daniel's news.

> **Karen's story:** Daniel is getting completely new office furniture, including a PC.
> **Lisa's story:** The sales department is having a makeover: new office furniture, new PCs, etc.
> **Pete's story:** They're going to completely redesign the office spaces and make it open plan.
> **Matt's story:** They're relocating the office miles away.

3 Ask students to listen again and tick the expressions that are used.

> Have you heard the news?   Guess what!   Do you know what?
> You won't believe this but ...   I've heard that ...   I don't believe it!
> Are you joking?   Really?   That's incredible!/unbelievable!
> That's fantastic!   Great!

Pronunciation
Expressing surprise

Go through the instructions and play the recording. Get students to listen and identify each pattern of intonation. Then ask them to listen again and repeat the expressions.

Speaking

Go through the *Expressions* list, particularly focusing on how to share a confidence as students have practised expressing interest in *Pronunciation*.

Go through the instructions with the class and get students to prepare by writing two more pieces of news. Get students to give and receive the news, using the intonation from *Pronunciation*.

It's my job

1 Ask students to discuss the questions. Round up at class level.

2 Ask students to read the datafile of *It's my job* and discuss what they know about marketing jobs. What do they think the job will involve? Ask students to read *It's my job* and make notes.

> **⚿** the company: a large company in New York, manufacturing personal care products such as soap, and specialist pet care products
>
> the responsibilities: marketing pet food, helping launch a new product, organizing market research, spent a month on a factory placement
>
> the workplace: friendly, part of a team, lots of training, flexi-time, finish early on Friday, presents at Christmas
>
> Ratana's ambition: wants to get a job there

Business know-how

1 Discuss annoying habits. Start students off by telling them what you find annoying. Then ask students to make a list of what they consider are annoying habits. Help them with the vocabulary they may need.

2 Ask students to read the list of irritating habits and compare it to their lists. Get them to put the list in order of class level and round up at class level.

Writing

Ask students to read the website and make notes of what skills, qualifications, etc. they need to apply for the internship using the list. Ask them to write a letter based on their notes. Get them to check that they have included everything asked for in the website.

➕ Additional activity

(all levels)

Have a class vote on the most irritating habits.

➕ Additional activity

(weaker students)

Ask students to read the website in *Writing* and answer these questions:

1 *What does WHO stand for?*

2 *What does it offer to interns?*

3 *What does WHO pay for?*

4 *What must you include in your application?*

➕ Writing bank

Letters 2: Covering letter – job application

Go to p.59 Student's Book.

11 Workplace skills

Background

Workplace skills, or **soft skills**, are increasingly becoming a key factor in gaining employment and advancing in a career. **Hard skills**, of course, remain important. These refer to the technical abilities needed to do a job and can be anything from understanding the technical specifications of a product to being able to produce a spreadsheet. But soft skills, such as the ability to work in a team, problem-solving, and self-motivation are now recognized as being of crucial importance.

So while hard skills focus on facts and knowledge, soft skills concentrate on feelings and behaviour. These include:

- **communication** – listening, making presentations, delegating, etc.
- **interaction** – handling conflicts, working in a team, giving and receiving feedback, etc.
- **self-management** – decision-making, stress management, willingness to learn, etc.
- **organization** – problem-solving, troubleshooting, etc.

Companies invest a lot of money in running soft skills courses in the knowledge that by improving the competencies of their workforce, they are giving their business a competitive edge. Courses may include effective listening, effective meetings, stress management, managing people, and negotiating skills. In the exploration of any of these areas, employees would be shown different strategies to improve their skills. So in the case of effective listening, specific tips might be:

- ask questions – show you are interested
- don't interrupt – relax and take time to listen
- respond to what you hear – e.g. *Yes, I see, Really?*, etc.
- ask clarifying questions, ask for examples
- don't guess what the person is feeling, listen instead
- avoid getting distracted by your surroundings

Employers place considerable importance on non-academic experience. Even though students leaving college will have little or no direct work experience, they will have developed some soft skills – the qualities and competencies that will make them more attractive candidates for any job.

✱ Tip

transferable skills the skills gathered through studies, various jobs, volunteer work, hobbies, sports, or other life experiences that can be used in your next job or new career.

➕ Additional activity

(weaker students)
Dictate these words and ask students to match the opposites. Get them to write definitions of each word with an example of what that person does.

*patient   thoughtful   generous
out-going   hard-working   reliable
funny   imaginative   sincere   decisive*

*thoughtless   insincere   indecisive
serious   impatient   unimaginative
lazy   mean   shy   unreliable*

If you are *patient*, you can wait for things and tolerate people who take a long time to do something.

Start up

1 Explain to the students that there are many skills which they already have from their studies and work which are 'transferable'. Explain to students what soft skills are, using the introduction to help you. Ask students to look at the headings and discuss with them what sort of activities they relate to in the workplace. Ask students to go though the questionnaire individually and tick one answer for each skill.

2 In pairs, get students to compare their results. At class level discuss what could be done to improve their skills.

Vocabulary

Personal qualities

1 Ask students to make a note of the personal qualities and personality words. Brainstorm other personality words with your students. Remind them of the words they learnt in Unit 4.

> ○╍ disorganized   persuasive   creative   logical   methodical
> well-organized

2 Ask students to work in pairs and decide on the most important qualities for each job.

➕ Additional activity

(weaker students)

Ask students to read the article again and list the places where they can develop soft skills.

(work experience, part-time jobs , working in a café or a shop, school or college, training courses at work, self-help courses, Internet)

✳ Tip

When students are using the Internet for research, encourage them to:
- simplify and summarize Information and not simply to copy chunks from the texts
- use *How to* (e.g. *How to manage your time*) as part of their search, as this will direct them to some useful sites

✳ Tip

Top margin p.80

Read the first quote: Ask students: *Do you agree with the advice from the employer?* Ask students to interpret the second quote (Communication skills are more important to employers than hard skills and knowledge.).

➕ Additional activity

(all levels)

Play the recording again after exercise 2 and ask students to make a note of the rules for building the bridge.

(Teams of four make the whole bridge, there must be supports for each end of the bridge and the horizontal span, it should have a minimum height of 20 cm from the floor, the winning team builds longest bridge. You can only use newspapers and sellotape and the bridge must be strong enough to support six bars of chocolate.)

➕ Grammar test

Go to p.92 Teacher's Resource Book.

Reading

1 Get students to read the first paragraph of the article and tell you what is wrong with Annie's behaviour and what soft skills she lacks.

2 Ask students to read the rest of the article and answer the questions.

> **⚷ 1** communication, listening effectively, working in a team, self-motivation, ability to organize your work, problem-solving, research skills, time management, influencing people, effective meetings, anger management, stress management, creativity
> **2, 3, 4** Students' own answers

Project

Ask students to work in pairs and research a soft skill area such as time management. Ask them to write a series of tips for their classmates.

Listening

1 Ask students to read the website and answer the questions.

> **⚷ 1** Team-building activities to help companies build their teams
> **2** Makes staff feel valued, improves communication, builds trust and helps company grow   **3** Students' own answers

2 Tell the class that they are going to hear a trainer for TEAM. Play the recording and ask students to tick the materials the teams can use.

> **⚷** Sellotape, newspaper, bars of chocolate

3 Go through the sentences before listening and ask students to guess the answers. Play the recording and ask students to do the matching exercise.

> **⚷ 1** c   **2** a   **3** d   **4** b

4 Play the recording again and ask students to answer the questions.

> **⚷ 1** Team 1 didn't test the bridge early enough; Team 2 didn't listen carefully enough to the rules; Team 3 kept changing their minds; Team 4 didn't plan well enough
> **2** Team 5 rolled up the paper into tubes, and stuck these together with the tape.

Language spot
Third Conditional

Ask students to read the rules and underline the imagined results in *Listening* exercise 3. Go through the Grammar reference with the students or set it as homework.

> **⚷** tested the bridge earlier; listened carefully to the rules; chosen a leader; had more time

1 Ask students to complete the sentences in class or for homework.

> 1 hadn't cancelled, would have been   2 would have sent, hadn't crashed
> 3 had talked, would have avoided   4 had taken, wouldn't have been
> 5 would have got behind, hadn't helped   6 had finished, wouldn't have missed

2 Get students to complete the sentences for themselves and then discuss them in pairs.

Reading

1 In pairs get students to discuss the questions.

2 Ask students to read the tips and complete them.

> 1 b   2 d   3 e   4 a   5 c

3 Ask students to read the tips again and choose one they could try out.

4 Ask students to work in groups and choose one of the discussion topics. Encourage them to use the tips.

Meeting room

Turn-taking

1 Ask students to look at the picture and tell you what is happening. Play the recording and ask students to answer the questions.

> 1 Spend £10,000 on charity   2 Decide the best thing to do with the money, choosing between a charity called Water Aid and a local theatre

2 Play the recording and get students to note the arguments in favour of the two proposals.

The charity proposal	The sponsorship proposal
The money will make a big impact.	Sponsorship is a good marketing tool.
2005–2015 is the 'Water for life' decade.	It will help the arts and the company.
The money will help a lot of people: £75 will train 10 people, £460 will pay for public water points, £1,000 will pay for a well.	People who go to the theatre are also potential readers. Makes link to the community stronger.

3 Go through the questions with the students and ask them to circle the names of the people.

> 2 Kim   3 Gianni   4 Emily   5 Kim

4 Go through the *Expressions* list and then play the recording and get students to number the expressions in the order they hear them.

> 1 What do you think?   2 Can I finish?   3 Sorry, I interrupted you.
> 4 Can I just say ...?   5 Do you have anything to add?
> 6 What do you think?   7 What's your opinion ...?

✱ Tip

thoughts: belief assumption judgment remember pay attention
emotions: feelings tone of voice reaction anger defensive
communication: say understand express explain interpretation

➕ Photocopiable activity
Difficult conversations
Go to p.93 Teacher's Resource Book.

✱ Tip

Top margin p.82
Ask students to cover the top margin. Then dictate the statistics to the class and then ask them to check their text. Ask them: *How often do you replace your mobile phone? Do you have a mobile phone in your house that no one uses?*

➕ Additional activity
(all levels)
Ask students to go through the expressions, labelling them A (inviting contributions), B (keeping talking), C (making a contribution) or D (apologizing for interrupting).

Speaking

1 Go through the task with the students carefully. Pre-teach: *clockwork, flat battery, inflatable, signal flare, insect repellent.*

2 Ask students to work alone and choose the ten most useful items in preparation for the speaking task.

3 Put the students in groups of four and ask them to agree on the ten most useful items. Round up at class level and decide on a class list.

Company profile

Nokia

1 Get students to work in pairs and discuss the questions.

2 Ask students to look at the photo and discuss what they know about the company e.g. *Where is it based?, How long has it been in business?, What else does it manufacture?* etc. Then read *Company profile* and answer the questions.

> 1 Helsinki, Finland; **Possible answer**: Because it makes it easier to run an international business, and Finnish is not spoken by many people outside Finland.
> 2 In the 1970s
> 3 The massive growth in the mobile phone industry created problems. **Possible answer**: because it wasn't prepared and couldn't grow quickly enough to deal with the competition
> 4 It provides equal opportunities and employee participation; people are encouraged to develop their personal skills and to help with the community.
> 5 **Possible answer:** Its solid background in telecommunications, its size, its belief in staff development, its investment in R & D, its core values based on customer satisfaction, its avoidance of bureaucracy

Business know-how

1 Ask students to read the tips about group work. Remind students that working in groups is like working in teams and developing teamwork skills is very important for the workplace.

2 Get students to discuss the tips in pairs, and decide which ones they already do and which they would like to try out.

Writing

Ask students to read the student's notes about their strengths. Ask them to tell you in each case: *What is the strength? What is the example the student gives?* Ask students to think of three strengths related to soft skills and ask them to make notes of a concrete example for each one. Tell them it is very important for any job application or interview that they have examples to back up their claims. Ask them to write up their notes as in the model.

➕ Additional activity
(weaker students)
Dictate the numbers, percentages and dates and ask students to try to remember what they refer to in *Company profile*. Ask students to check their answers in the article.
34%   1865   1966   1980s   80%
1990s   2006 $5 billion   60,000

➕ Writing bank
Notes and messages
Go to p.60 Student's Book.

12 Presentations

Background

Presentations are acts of communication where a speaker addresses an audience to convey certain information. At any one time, tens of thousands of presentations are taking place in offices, meeting rooms, and auditoria. They form an essential part of the working lives of all employees, either as members of the audience or as speakers.

Presentations can range from formal high-tech events to hundreds of people to simply reporting back to colleagues at an informal departmental meeting. Whatever the situation, they have distinct advantages over written communications or unstructured spoken interaction:

- they allow two-way communication. People can ask questions and the speaker can check understanding
- the speaker can assess the reaction of the audience and adapt the presentation accordingly, e.g. if the audience looks doubtful, the speaker can present information with more commitment, positive arguments, etc.
- body language and visual aids make an impact on the audience
- variety can be introduced by moving between talking, visual aids (e.g. PowerPoint), and the asking and taking of questions

- the speaker has control over the order and flow of information, and therefore over the audience.

Before preparing a presentation, some basic questions need to be answered.

- **Why** is it happening? Is it to present information? To sell a product or service? To sell ideas? etc.
- **What** are the key messages? Research shows that audiences don't absorb more than four or five key points.
- **Who** is the audience? A presentation must be tailored to the expectations and needs of the participants.

Presentations are sometimes stressful affairs, either because of the importance of the event, or simply because addressing colleagues or managers can be nerve-wracking. However, like any other aspect of our working lives, there are basic skills which can be learnt or improved. The key to any successful presentation is **preparation**, which involves:

- planning: structuring the talk, preparing notes, etc.
- designing and preparing visual aids (PowerPoint, etc)
- rehearsing, timing, and revising the presentation.

✚ Additional activity

(all levels)

As preparation for this unit, ask students to prepare a two-minute talk about something they know a lot about: their hobby, a country, a festival, etc. Tell them that you want them to give talks to the class before doing the work in the unit, so they can compare their own performance now with how it changes as they learn more about giving a presentation. Ask them to give their talks to small groups of about five or six students. Students should write notes about the talk: one good thing about it, and one less successful thing about it.

Start up

1 Ask students to work in groups and discuss the questions.

2 Look at the pictures with the students and then play the recording. Ask students to put the pictures in order.

> **O⟁** 1 d   2 f   3 a   4 b   5 c   6 e

3 Ask students to make a note of what they think the speaker is doing wrong in each case. As you go through the problems discuss them with the students – what can be done to avoid the problem, if they have ever been to a talk that had the same problem, etc.

> **O⟁** a putting too much on a slide   b taking too long / managing timing badly   c being unprepared   d reading from notes
> e closing badly   f speaking too quietly

➕ Additional activity
(all levels)
Ask students to cover the website and try to answer these questions in pairs.
How many points do people remember easily?
Why divide your talk into threes?
Why does a good quote or anecdote help?
How many typefaces should you use?
Why avoid capital letters?
Why use lots of visuals?
Why wear smart clothes?
What should you check?
What does K I S S mean?
How does breathing deeply help?
How should you speak?

✳ Tip
For the rest of the course, encourage students to give talks where possible and make sure that all students in the class have an opportunity to talk. You can also team weak students with strong students and have two students give a talk together, to help the weaker student gain confidence.

✳ Tip
Top margin p.86
Ask students to work in pairs and read about *Dragon's Den*. Ask them to discuss these questions:
● *What do you think of reality TV?*
● *Have you seen any programmes similar to this?*

✳ Tip
pitch the set of activities designed to persuade someone to buy a product.
tips for pitching
● have the answers
● prepare
● catch their attention
The elevator pitch
You are in an elevator with a potential employer and you have to tell him or her about your strengths in a minute. What would you say?

➕ Grammar test
Go to p.94 Teacher's Resource Book.

➕ Additional activity
(all levels)
Ask students to visit the *Dragons' Den* website and find out about different projects: www.bbc.co.uk/dragonsden. Ask them to find out about the dragons and what their backgrounds are and to find out what the ideas were in 2006.

Vocabulary
Presentation accessories
Ask students to match the accessories with the definitions. Ask students if they have ever used any of these aids in a talk. Encourage students to use some of these aids for the work in this unit, even if only whiteboards and markers or visual aids that they hold up.

> 🔑 1 e 2 a 3 h 4 c 5 g 6 d 7 b 8 f

Reading
1 Ask students to discuss the questions, and round up at class level.

2 Get students to read the article and complete it.

> 🔑 1 easily 2 variety 3 interesting 4 visuals 5 read 6 content
> 7 nervous 8 effective 9 confident 10 directly 11 avoid
> 12 communicate

3A Ask students to prepare a two-minute talk about something they know a lot about. (If they gave a talk at the beginning of this unit, they can talk about the same topic again or choose another topic.)

3B Ask students to bring visuals from home or find them online if there is time. Otherwise ask them to give the talk without visuals. Encourage them to think of a story to tell about their topic. Get them to copy the form and take it in turns to give their talk. The other student should make notes in the form. Afterwards they should give feedback to each other. (If they gave a talk at the beginning of the unit, they can compare their performance with their first attempt.)

4 Ask students to give their talks to the class. Not everyone needs to give a talk this time. Students can give feedback on their partner's talk.

Listening
1 Ask students what they know about people who go sailing and keep yachts in marinas. *What sort of people are they? What sort of Internet access do you think they would like?* Play the recording with the page covered up and ask students: *How many investors are there? What is the company called? What does it provide? What sort of people would buy this service?* Then go through the datafile with the students before they listen again. Play the recording and ask students to complete it.

> 🔑 1 Internet 2 sailing 3 business 4 connection 5 fixed
> 6 75,000

2 Go through the sentences with the students before they listen. Play the recording and ask students to correct the errors.

> 🔑 2 25,000 not 2,500 paying customers. 3 She started it two years ago not three years ago. 4 She said she had signed up 40 marinas not 50.
> 5 She said she could attract advertisers to the website not customers.
> 6 Sam offered £75,000 not £65,000.

Language spot

Reported speech 1: *said*, *told*, and questions

Go through the grammar with the students. Ask them to look at the sentences in *Listening*, exercise 2 and get them to discover what happened to the verbs. Ask students to also notice how the pronouns change.

> 🔑 cost   could attract   would offer   was going to generate   had started

Go through the Grammar reference with students or set as homework.

Ask students to report the extracts using the correct verb.

> 🔑 1 Asma said that the marina provided a base for the equipment.
> 2 Sam asked if she was very successful.
> 3 Asma told them that they were planning to target more marinas that year.
> 4 Asma said that they couldn't grow the business without extra investment.
> 5 Louise asked what they knew about boating.
> 6 Alessandro told her that it was the best pitch that he had seen in a long time.
> 7 Asma said that she had developed the idea when she was studying at college.
> 8 Asma told them that it was a deal.

Speaking

1 Ask students to look at the list of eight ideas. Then divide them into groups (if you have enough students, have a maximum of eight groups, otherwise have fewer) and allocate an idea to each group.
Each group decides on answers to the seven items in the dark blue box. Encourage students to use the language of turn-taking in Unit 11.

2 Get the groups to prepare a presentation with visuals for their idea. They should give each member of the group something to say.

3 Go through the rules, 'How to enter *The Lions' Cave*' with the students. They cannot invest less than £50,000 in a project. Go through the *Expressions* list with the students before they start their pitches.

It's my job

1 Ask students to discuss the question in pairs.

2 Get students to read *It's my job* and answer the questions.

> 🔑 1 She goes to gigs in the evening, and works at weekends   2 People skills, telephone techniques, good relationships with the artists, market knowledge, communication skills, presentation skills   3 She has to make presentations to company executives and present company plans to the artists   4 She understands the worries and concerns of the artists. Possible other advantages include knowing about music, knowing musicians, being musical so being a good judge of talent, etc.

➕ Photocopiable activity
Presentations – FAQs
Go to p.95 Teacher's Resource Book.

✳ Tip

Top margin p.88
Go through the business buzzwords with the students. Ask them to match these definitions to each buzzword:
be creative and think beyond boundaries (*think outside the box*)
a number that is near the total, that you can use for discussion (*ball park figure*)
be challenging, do something to the maximum possible (*push the envelope*)
make sure that people are informed (*keep in the loop*)
make sure that someone who doesn't know about a project is informed about it (*bring up to speed*)
establish contact with someone or renew a line of communication (*touch base*)

➕ Additional activity
(all levels)

Ask students why they think Karen is a bit depressed in the final conversation.

Small talk
Bad news

1 Ask students to look at the picture and think about how Karen and Daniel are feeling.

2 Pre-teach *computer crashed, closed down, went dead/fallen through*. Play the recording and ask the students to answer the questions.

> 1 His computer crashed and he lost his presentation.
> 2 Because he has to see his boss, who isn't happy.
> 3 A deal with an important client has fallen through.
> 4 Her promotion depended on it.

3 Go through the *Expressions* list and then play the recording and get students to number the expressions in the order they hear them.

> 1 I had a real disaster   2 Oh no   3 That's terrible   4 I'm so sorry
> 5 I got some bad news   6 I'm really sorry to hear that
> 7 You poor thing

Pronunciation
/ əʊ / and / ɒ /

Play the recording and ask students to underline the /əʊ/ sounds and circle the /ɒ/ sounds. Then play the recording again for students to repeat the sentences.

> 1 Oh no! It's John on the phone.
> 2 I'm so sorry. What will you do now?
> 3 She got a terrible shock.
> 4 Why won't you ask for a promotion?
> 5 Who do you want to go to the show?

✳ Tip

agenda a list of what is going to be discussed in the meeting
minutes the formal notes written after the meeting
chair / chairperson the person who directs the meeting formally
secretary the person who makes notes during the meeting
action points points made during the meeting that individuals have to do
a motion a formal point made by someone in a meeting
to second a motion when someone formally says that they will support a motion. This is necessary for a motion to be voted on.
to carry a motion if the people in the meeting vote in favour of a meeting

➕ Additional activity

Ask students to work in pairs and discuss what the qualities of a good 'chairperson' are.

➕ Writing bank
Agendas and Minutes

Go to p.62 Student's Book.

Speaking

Go through the *Expressions* list again and explain the activity. Ask students to read their roles before they start and prepare what they are going to say by answering the questions and making notes. The students take it in turns to tell their stories and use expressions of sympathy.

Business know-how

1 Ask the class to discuss the questions.

2 In pairs get students to read the tips and decide on the most important ones. Then ask students to discuss their choices with another pair.

Writing

Go through the activity with the class. Brainstorm ideas with the class following the points in the book. Then ask students to write a handout individually or in pairs. Ask them to follow the instructions.

13 Big business

Background

Most larger businesses are private or public **limited companies** (or **corporations** in the US). They have a minimum of two **shareholders**, i.e. investors who own **shares** in the company. Shareholders receive the profits of the company as **dividends**, paid to them in proportion to the amount they have invested. If the business fails, the owners have **limited liability** and only lose the amount they have invested in the business, unlike a sole trader or partnership where the owner(s) has **unlimited liability** for all the debts. To become a public limited company, a private company is **floated** by the issuing of shares.

A **private limited company**
- is identified by the abbreviation 'Ltd' after the name
- is often a family business whose owners are both shareholders and directors
- cannot be quoted on the Stock Exchange
- can only sell shares if all the shareholders agree

A **public limited company**
- is the largest kind of business
- is identified by the letters 'plc' after the name
- has shares which are normally traded on the Stock Exchange
- has shares owned by members of the public and institutional investors (e.g. banks or pension funds)
- can raise funds to develop or expand the company by issuing shares

Multinational companies (or **transnational companies**) are defined by the UN as 'associations which possess and control means of production or services outside the country in which they were established'. They are the giants of the business world. PepsiCo, for example, is the world's largest drinks company with more than 500 factories in over 100 countries and employing 335,000 workers. Nestlé, the Swiss food manufacturer, has more than 200,000 employees located in 126 countries.

Multinationals enjoy certain benefits due to their size and global reach, including:
- economies of scale
- avoiding local taxes and duties
- reducing tax bills by declaring their profits in a country with low taxation
- global access to capital and investment
- the ability to move their business to countries with lower costs
- spreading risk by operating in different markets

Multinationals are sometimes criticized for the extent of their economic (and possibly political) power and for 'exploiting' the workforce and natural resources of the developing world.

✚ Additional activity
(all levels)
Ask students to work in pairs and think of other examples of business strengths, weaknesses, opportunities and threats. Round up at class level.

Start up

1 Ask students to read the information and answer the questions.

> 🔑 to know what is happening in their business and the world, to measure performance, plan future strategies
>
> by understanding strengths and weaknesses they can change to improve their performance, by looking at threats and opportunities they can plan strategies for the future

2 Ask students to prepare a SWOT analysis for themselves by answering the questions. Ask students to work in pairs and talk about their SWOT analyses. Encourage them to help each other think of other ideas they may not have thought of.

Listening

Ask students to guess what the opportunities and threats may be for this business sector. Play the recording and get students to make notes.

> **⊙━ Strengths**
> hold stocks of specialist goods
> good sources of supply
> fast efficient delivery
> strong commitment to online operation
> **Weaknesses**
> not in wider market
> not enough knowledge of foreign markets
> difficult to deliver orders if demand were high
> **Opportunities**
> ability to build brand name
> offer products and services, e.g. music downloads
> **Threats**
> competitors may offer a better, faster service

Language spot

Verbs + *to* or verb + *-ing*

Ask students to read the rules and ask students to come up with appropriate verbs to link with the verbs in the lists, e.g. *afford to buy / to invest / to purchase; dare to think / to invest / to offer* etc. Go through the Grammar reference or set it for homework.

1 Ask students to read through the texts before they try to complete the gaps. Ask them: *What has Denis O'Brian done? Who has Best Buy teamed up with?* Get students to complete the articles and compare their answers in pairs.

> **⊙━** 1 to open   2 to create   3 to provide   4 to expand   5 to walk out
> 6 to freeze   7 to withdraw

2 Ask students to complete the sentences for homework or in class.

> **⊙━** 1 trying   2 giving   3 thinking of   4 meeting/to meet
> 5 to achieve   6 to attend   7 delaying   8 to get

3 Ask students to complete the sentences for themselves and compare their answers in groups.

Vocabulary

Business terms

Get students to work in pairs and match the definitions with the words in the article.

> **⊙━** 2 capital   3 duties   4 board of directors   5 policies   6 debts
> 7 Stock Exchange   8 shares   9 turnover   10 shareholder

➕ Grammar test
Go to p.96 Teacher's Resource Book.

✱ Tip
Short news reports and headlines often use verb phrases with *to* or *-ing*.
The infinitive is often used to talk about the future, e.g. *easyJet to buy new planes* in newspaper headlines.

➕ Additional activity
(stronger students)
Take in a selection of business magazines and newspapers. Ask students to find examples of verb + *-ing*, verb + *to* and the infinitive to talk about the future.

✱ Tip
Top margin p.92
Ask students to look at the information about the London Stock Exchange. Can they find out similar information about the New York Stock Exchange?

➕ Additional activity

(stronger students)

Ask students to read the following and work in groups to decide if they refer to Private Limited Companies or Public Limited Companies. Students have to use their understanding of the difference between the two types of companies to guess the answers.

1 they cannot be quoted on the Stock Exchange (*private*)
2 their shares can be sold with no restrictions (*public*)
3 their shares can only be sold when all the shareholders agree (*private*)
4 their shares are sold on the Stock Exchange (*public*)
5 they are usually owned by the entrepreneurs who created the company (*private*)
6 most of their shares are owned by large organizations (*public*)

➕ Additional activity

(all levels)

Before *Speaking* get students to brainstorm as many multinational companies as they can. Magazines and newspapers will provide a lot of ideas for students, if they look at the adverts and read the business quotations.

Get students to work in pairs discussing which companies they have heard of and what business areas they operate in.

✳ Tip

Top margin p.94

Ask students to work in pairs and discuss the question: *Do you agree with Soichiro Honda about recruitment? Is this also true of building teams? What does the second quote mean?*

✳ Tip

Encourage students to use intonation to express certainty or uncertainty. Play the recording again and get students to copy the intonation of the sentences.

Reading

1 Ask students to read the first paragraph and answer the questions.

> ⚷ 1 People can invest in the company without having unlimited responsibility for any debts.
> 2 the board of directors
> 3 Shares go up when a company is doing well and down if the company is doing badly.
> 4 They get a share of the profits.

2 Ask students to read the statements and decide if they are true or false.

> ⚷ 1 F 2 F 3 T 4 T 5 F 6 T 7 F 8 T

Speaking

1 Ask students to read about company A and to guess what famous multinational company it could be. Go through the instructions and the example with the students. Ask students to read the information in groups and discuss what multinational companies they could be.

> ⚷ A Google B Coca-Cola C Sony D Microsoft E Honda
> F Intel G Nokia H McDonald's

2 Get students to work in pairs and to describe multinational companies to each other. They can ask questions and should try to guess what they are.

Meeting room

Expressing certainty, probability, and possibility

1 Ask students to look at the picture and answer the questions.

2 Play the recording and ask students: *What are they talking about?* (whether they will reach the sales targets). Then go through the *Expressions* list with the students. Play the recording again and ask students to identify how sure each of the people is about achieving their sales target.

> ⚷ Laura: S   Jamie: S   Yusuf: NVS

3 Play the recording and ask students: *What are they talking about?* (the magazine being taken over). Then play the recording again and ask students to identify how sure the people are.

> ⚷ Laura: S   Jamie: FS   Kim: FS   Yusuf: NVS

Speaking

Ask students to work in groups and discuss the topics in the list. Encourage them to use the *Expressions* list.

+ Additional activity
(weaker students)
Ask students to close their books. Dictate these sentences, and ask students to tell you if you are sure, fairly sure or not very sure.

1 *Computers are bound to become smaller and more powerful.*
2 *Sales of CDs are likely to fall in the next few years.*
3 *The use of Blackberrys will definitely increase.*
4 *I don't think that Microsoft will lose control of the market.*
5 *We may not travel by plane as much as in the past.*
6 *I expect that we will have folding keyboards and tiny laptops in the future.*

Company profile
Honda

1 If possible take in photos of Honda products and show them to your students. Ask students to work in pairs and discuss the questions.

2 Ask students to work in pairs. Divide them into As and Bs. Each student has different information about Honda. Student A reads the text on page 94 and Student B reads the text on page 113.

When they have read and understood their questions ask them to find out the answers to their questions from their partner.

What products does Honda develop? racing motorcycles, Formula One cars, robots
How successful is Honda? It is growing, especially in Asia and Europe – it is not as big as Toyota. It made $5 billion in 2007.
Why is Honda successful? technically innovative, flexible, low production costs, successful marketing strategies, memorable advertising campaigns, invests in research and development
What is Honda's philosophy? sharing its 'dream', making its workplace safe, fair and diverse, conducting business ethically, invests in many projects to help the wider community
What does Honda make? cars, trucks, motorcycles, scooters, watercraft, engines, garden equipment, aeronautical and mobile technologies
Where is Honda based? headquarters are in Tokyo. American branch is based in California, big company in Canada, and other countries
How did Honda start? founded in Japan in 1948 by Soichiro Honda providing basic transport, fitting engines to bicycles, and then scooters and motorcycles
How did it develop into a multinational company? by the 1970s Honda was largest motorcycle producer in the world, produced cars in 1960 for the Japanese market, but in 1970s introduced a new economical range of cars worldwide, became the first Japanese car manufacturer to build plants in the USA

* Tip
For the *Project*, encourage students to use their knowledge of the world to think about competitors of the company and to research those companies as well. Ask students to use the links and read articles about the company to help them build up a balanced picture of the company and its economic environment. It is not enough to simply use the website of the company itself.

+ Photocopiable activity
Multinationals
Go to p.97 Teacher's Resource Book.

+ Writing bank
Reports 2 – Describing trends
Go to p.56 Student's Book.

Business know-how

1 Ask students to read the problem and discuss in pairs how they would deal with it.

2 Ask students to read and discuss the tips. Which ones do they do already? At class level ask students to choose the three most useful tips.

Project

Ask students to choose a large company, preferably a multinational. Get them to do research on the net, making notes in a SWOT table.

Students can also present their findings to the class.

Writing

Ask students to write a simple report about the company using the table as a plan. Each category can be a paragraph. They should write a final paragraph with their conclusions and recommendations.

14 Entrepreneurs

Background

An **entrepreneur** is defined as 'a person who makes money by starting or running businesses, especially when this involves taking financial risks'.

Three of the business world's greatest entrepreneurs today started young. Michael Dell started his company, Dell, while he was still a student at the University of Texas. Bill Gates started Microsoft while he was an undergraduate at Harvard. Richard Branson, whose Virgin Group is an $8 billion global business made up of some 200 companies in 30 countries, was only 15 when he launched a magazine called *Student*.

Major business schools and universities in the US now offer courses for budding entrepreneurs.

- 900 MBA students take an entrepreneurship course in their first semester at Harvard University, Mass.
- the University of Colorado has a 'green' entrepreneurship programme helping students to create eco-friendly companies

- the University of Texas speeds up the creation of start-up companies by offering students technology, office space and access to specialist advisors. Over 60 companies have already been launched.

However, not all young entrepreneurs follow the business school path.

- Liz Jackson had little education, no funds and no property to secure a loan. But at the age of 25 she launched Great Guns Marketing, a telemarketing company, in the lounge of her flat. It now employs 100 people and has a turnover of $1.5 million.
- Alex Tew set up The Million Dollar Homepage at the age of 21. This simply offers a logo and a link on the page for $1 a pixel. But by selling this advertising space, he became a dollar millionaire in just a few months.
- In 2004, at the age of 21, James Murray Wells started Glasses Direct, offering reading glasses for £15 a pair. In 2005, he sold 22,000 pairs and was named Entrepreneur of the Year by Startups.co.uk.

Start up

1 Ask students to look at the list and decide how much they spend on each one. Ask them to make a note of any other things they spend their money on.

2 Ask students to work in pairs and compare their spending patterns. Encourage them to discuss the different areas. Round up at class level.

Vocabulary

Personal money

Ask students to complete the sentences.

Oⲧ	1 interest	2 withdraw	3 statement	4 bank loan	5 credit card
	6 deposits	7 cheques	8 overdraft	9 exchange rates	
	10 receipts				

Listening

1 Ask students to look at the photo. *Who are the people? What do they do?* Play the recording and ask students to answer the question.

> Oⲧ It is Sophie's first job and she has a low salary and large debts from university. She finds it difficult to manage her spending.

➕ Additional activity

(stronger students)
Ask students to research bank accounts online. Get them to compare two current accounts and decide which one offers the best deal. Suggest they look at: interest rates for overdrafts, number of cash points, cost of running the account, etc. Possible accounts: first direct, Nationwide, Goldfish, Premier Direct, cahoot, smile.

✳ Tip

entrepreneur a person who starts a new business or venture and who is responsible for the risks involved.

➕ Photocopiable activity
Managing a budget
Go to p.99 Teacher's Resource Book.

2 Get students to work in pairs and think about the advice Liam might give for each area.

3 Play the recording and get students to complete the advice.

O–ᴛ	Outgoings	Liam's advice
	saving	save regularly in case there's an unexpected expense
	credit card	cut it up; it's quick to get into debt and the interest rates are high
	shopping	avoid going shopping, go to factory outlets
	lunch	make own sandwiches
	going out	go to bars with special midweek prices, restaurants with fixed price menus, have friends round and make a simple meal and watch a DVD
	travelling to work	buy a bike and travel around free

4 Ask students to work in pairs and discuss the advice. Encourage them to offer other ideas. Round up at class level.

Reading

1 Get students to look at the photos and read the headlines. Ask students to read the article and answer the questions.

> O–ᴛ 1 It helps young people aged between 16 and 30 to set up their own businesses.
> 2 He set up his own record label.
> 3 She designs wallpapers and fabrics.
> 4 She worked as a brand manager and business consultant.
> 5 Because there are no local competitors.

2 Ask students to work in pairs and discuss the questions.

3 Ask students to translate the terms into their own language.

Language spot
Defining and non-defining relative clauses

Ask students to read the rules. Go through the Grammar reference or set it for homework.

1 Get students to do the activity and discuss their answers at class level.

> O–ᴛ **Defining**
> LiveWIRE offers awards which recognize the best ...
> She designs wallpaper and fabrics which have been commissioned ...
> ... she decided to set up a business which sells natural handmade skincare products.

✳ Tip

Top margin p.98
Ask students to read the quotes in pairs. Ask each pair to paraphrase the quotes so they can explain them to the rest of the class.

Ask students to complete the sentences:
A successful entrepreneur ...
To be an entrepreneur you have to ...
Being an entrepreneur is like ...

✚ Additional activity

(all levels)
Ask students to read the article again and answer the questions:
1 How does Shell help young entrepreneurs?
2 Name some other countries apart from Britain it operates in.
3 Who is Black Ivory Records' first artist? How has the award helped Robert?
4 Where did Johanna study? What is her work experience? How is the award going to help her?

✳ Tip

access the opportunity or right to use something
set up to create something, such as a business, or start it
spot to see or notice someone or something when it is not easy to do so
placement a job where you get some experience of a particular kind of work
commission a formal request to somebody to design or make a piece of work
mentor an experienced person who advises and helps somebody with less experience over a period of time

➕ Grammar test

Go to p.98 Teacher's Resource Book.

➕ Additional activity

(all levels)

Ask students to vote on the ideas which are on the page, both the three businesses in the article and the ideas of Anthony Eskinazi, Matt Roberts and Irfan Badakshi and Alex Tew.

Alternatively get them to do more research about each idea and find out if the businesses continue to be successful.

Non-defining

His label, which is called Black Ivory Records, has one artist …

… and spends his time in the studio, where he rehearses, composes and arranges his music.

His first solo album, which was spotted by a major record company in the USA, was a great success.

Johanna, who is a Scottish art school graduate, set up …

She had placements at various London design studios, where she realized …

Her wallpaper, which is inspired by nature, was used by …

Wajeeha Khan, who graduated with an MBA from Lahore University, went into business …

She has manufactured and launched her products in Pakistan, where there are no local competitors.

She was selected by the organization, …, which is called the Tameer Entrepreneurial Club, as a role model …

---

2 Get students to write the sentences in class or as homework.

O— 1 Anthony has an innovative idea which helps people find a parking space in their area.
2 He has a free website where people can advertise their parking spaces.
3 He has a website which already has 50,000 'hits' a day.

3 Look at the picture with your students and discuss the product. Get students to write the sentences in class or as homework.

O— 1 Matt Roberts and Irfan Badakshi, who realized partygoers needed a place to sleep, developed a soft chair that changes into a bed.
2 Alex Tew, who was still a student, created a website in 2005.
3 The website, which is called The Million Dollar Homepage, made more than a million dollars in five months.

➕ Additional activity

(all levels)

When students have written their reports for the *Project*, ask them to put up their reports around the room or distribute them in photocopies. Have a class discussion about the qualities and skills needed to run and set up your own business.

✱ Tip

Top margin p.100

Ask students to read and discuss the advice and then vote on the thing they would prefer to give up.

➕ Additional activity

(all levels)

Play the recordings for *Small talk* again and ask students to make a note of how:
● Angela and Gary ask Karen to do something
Could you possibly work late this evening?
Do you fancy seeing it some time?
● Angela and Gary answer Karen when she says no to their requests:
Don't worry about it. Really. That's OK. No worries.

Project

Get students to work in pairs and choose an entrepreneur to research. It could be a world-famous person like the founder of Ryanair or easyJet or an entrepreneur famous in the students' own country or region. Ask them to make notes in the areas listed. Then get them to write a report on the person, using the areas as guidelines for sections of the report.

Small talk

Compliments and saying 'no'

1 Play the recording and ask students to answer the questions.

O— 1 her report   2 work late in the evening; no   3 her top
4 going to see a film

2 Play the recording and ask students to answer the questions.

> **⊙—** 1 to the cinema   2 it was a birthday present from Daniel

3 Get students to listen again and tick the expressions.

> **⊙—** Do you really think so?   That's really nice to hear.   That's very kind of you.   I'd love to but I'm afraid I can't.

Speaking

Go through the *Expressions* list with the students again. Ask students to work in pairs. Then go through the task with the students making sure they understand that there are two stages to the conversation. If necessary play the dialogue between Angela and Karen again as a model.

➕ Additional activity

(all levels)

Ask students to read the article again and then get them to cover it up. Then ask them these questions.

1 *What made Kasem choose a job in banking?*
2 *What important purchase does he help people with?*
3 *What gives him most satisfaction?*
4 *What part of the job does he like least?*

It's my job

1 Ask students what duties bank workers have. Then ask them to read *It's my job* quickly to check their answers.

2 Ask students to discuss the question.

> **⊙— Possible answer**
> He really wants to help people, he is well-trained, he gets satisfaction from helping people, he treats people well.

Business know-how

1 Go through the instructions with the students and ask them to rate themselves for each quality.

2 Ask students to work in pairs and discuss their results. Ask students to report to the class whether they have similar or different results.

➕ Writing bank
Memos
Go to p.55 Student's Book.

Writing

Go through the instructions and ask students to write the emails. They then swap them and answer the email turning down the requests.

> **⊙— Possible answer**
>
> I'm just writing to say that you gave a very good sales presentation last week. I thought it was very clear and enjoyable. Some foreign visitors are coming to the office next Thursday afternoon and I wondered if you would be able to give the same presentation to them.
>
> It's very kind of you to say that you enjoyed my sales presentation. Unfortunately, I am not able to give the presentation to the visitors next Thursday as I am out of the office on that day. I hope that you find someone to help.

15 Job hunting

Background

There are a number of ways that young people can improve their chances of getting a job.

- To begin with, job seekers have to find potential or actual job vacancies. Being **pro-active** creates possibilities. Rather than simply waiting for advertisements to appear, they should actively look for unadvertised opportunities and make use of personal connections. Employers like a get-up-and-go attitude.
- **Research** is essential both for exploring job possibilities and for improving prospects with applications and interviews. The most successful applications are the result of careful preparation on what the job involves, what is happening in the sector, and who the competitors are.
- Job seekers should **speak to people** in the business and consult careers services. In this way they can learn more about the career they are interested in and how they can get ahead. They can also ask for informational (rather than specific job) interviews with companies.
- If still at college, they should gain work experience and get involved in extra-curricular activities. Employers like to see people who '**have a life**' and make the most of their time.

- They should keep **a 'beginner's mind'**. Employers want to see people who are open, adaptable and willing to learn, not people who think they already know it all.

A **CV**, with its accompanying covering letter, is a key document for making an impact with potential employers. The best CVs:

- are clear, interesting and concise. Job seekers should always keep in mind that a CV has one essential function – to get them an interview
- 'sell' the applicant to employers. The **profile** should tell them about the applicant's skills, qualities and experience – and be adapted for specific jobs
- are easy-to-read, clearly laid-out, and accurate. An application with spelling and grammatical errors will be immediately rejected.

The **covering letter** has the essential function of ensuring that a CV is read. Recruitment consultants and employers read hundreds of applications, so a covering letter acts as a kind of advertisement for the CV. While highlighting the job seeker's key strengths relevant to the job – it should be brief, enthusiastic, and interesting. And as with the CV, accurate!

➕ Additional activity

(weaker students)
As preparation for *Start up* ask students to brainstorm personality adjectives. Then get them to brainstorm the sort of jobs that are available to them in their town or city. Write their ideas on the board.

➕ Additional activity

(stronger students)
As a follow up for *Start up*, ask students to write four paragraphs about their key areas.

Start up

1 Go through the form with the students and check that they understand all the skill areas and key areas. Explain the form carefully.

2 Ask students to think of a personal example for each key area that they circled.

3 Get students to compare their answers in pairs. They should ask questions about the personal examples.

4 Get students to think about what their partner has told them and to suggest suitable careers. Round up at class level. Get students to say what jobs they have recommended for their partners and why.

➕ Additional activity
(all levels)
Ask students to listen again and answer these questions:
Step 2 What should you remember to include in your list?
Step 3 What do universities and colleges organize? How can they be useful? Why can networking be effective? What should you prepare?
Step 4 Why are temporary jobs useful?
Ask students to read the advice in the tapescript on page 130.

➕ Grammar test
Go to p 100 Teacher's Resource Book.

✳ Tip
Top margin p.104
Go through the interview questions with the students and ask them why they think they are strange or inappropriate questions.

➕ Additional activity
(all levels)
Round up at class level. You could get the class to vote on the best solutions for each problem or scenario.

✳ Tip
Explain to students that there are no correct answers to these situations. If you have monolingual classes, your students may be tempted to speak in their own language in this activity. Encourage them to continue speaking in English.

Listening

1 Ask students to discuss the question in groups.

> **Oₙ Possible answers**
> CV writing   Job seeking   Answering questions
> Researching a company   Presenting yourself effectively, etc.

2 Go through the instructions with the students and ask them to complete the rules of successful job seeking.

> **Oₙ** *Step 1* find out what employers want.   *Step 2* understand yourself.
> *Step 3* actively seek for a job.   *Step 4* make yourself more employable.
> *Step 5* stay positive.

3 Play the recording again and ask students just to listen for the advice in the list. Then ask them to match the advice with the steps. Play the recording again and get students to check their answers.

> **Oₙ** b 2   c 4   d 1   e 3   f 5   g 4

Language spot
Reported speech 2: orders and advice

Ask students to read and complete the rules. Go through the Grammar reference with students or set it for homework.

> **Oₙ** 1 told   2 had to   3 advised

1 Get students to report the five steps orally and write sentences for homework.

> **Oₙ** He told them they had to understand themselves.
> He told them they had to actively seek for a job.
> He told them they had to make themselves more employable.
> He told them they had to stay positive.

2 Ask students to choose five examples of Duncan's advice, and write sentences using *advised*.

Reading

Get students to read the introduction and answer the questions.

> **Oₙ** 1 You are asked to solve a problem or to discuss a business scenario.
> 2 To test your quick thinking and intelligence.
> 3 Your logical thinking, general knowledge, insight and knowledge, performance under pressure, creativity and communication skills.
> 4 Students' own answers.

Speaking

1 Divide the students into groups of three. If possible mix up students with different strengths. Ask students to work through the problems and scenarios, making a note of their decisions in each case.

2 Put two or three groups together to compare their ideas. Make sure they justify their ideas to the other groups.

3 Ask students which tasks they found easier and more difficult. Ask students to tell you what tools and strategies they used to do the activities. Go through the list and find out which ones your students preferred. Discuss with them which methods are best for which type of problem.

Project

In pairs get students to read the business scenario and discuss it, using the guidelines. If possible they should use the Internet to find out about the sports shoe business and its key markets, making notes of relevant information. Encourage students to make use of the thinking skills discussed in *Speaking*, exercise 3. Ask students to write a short report for the company offering advice for its future marketing strategies. Alternatively ask students to prepare a presentation for the class.

Meeting room

Dealing with difficult conversations

1 Get students to discuss the question.

Possible answers
her performance on recent jobs, her training needs, her future projects, her ambitions, her opinion of the team, her ideas for how the team could work better, etc.

2 Play the recording and ask students to answer the questions.

1 the importance of accuracy, checking and re-checking information, meeting deadlines and keeping to schedules, and that the job can be stressful
2 the launch of the new format of the magazine; working well as a team and giving each other support.
3 effective meetings skills

3 Play the recording again and get students to tick the expressions they hear.

I'm not sure I've understood the question. What do you mean by...?
That's a good / interesting / important question. It's difficult to say.
Let me see / think... That's a good point.

* Tip

Top margin p.106
Tell students that Ricardo Semler is the CEO of a highly successful business. Ask students to discuss the two quotes. In what way does he seem unusual in his approach?

* Tip

appraisal a formal meeting with your manager to discuss your performance and plan future tasks

Additional activity

(all levels)
Play the recording again and ask students to answer these questions.

1 *Does Kim consider any of her past year too stressful?*
2 *Why couldn't Kim go on training courses in the past six months?*

Speaking

Go through the *Expressions* list with the class, asking them to repeat the sentences after you, paying attention to pronunciation and intonation. Go through the speaking activity instructions with the students. Get students to have the discussion in pairs. Encourage them to use expressions for buying time and asking for clarification, and to try and keep the conversation going naturally.

Company profile
Semco

1 Ask students to imagine they are the managers of a large company and to discuss the question in pairs. Round up at class level.

2 Pre-teach: *machinery, manufacturer, recession, productivity, defect, rotate, bonus.* Ask students to read the *Company profile* and try to guess what words could fit in the gaps. Then get them to work in pairs and complete the article. Did they guess correctly?

> **1** traditional **2** disagreed **3** fired **4** teams **5** costs
> **6** profits **7** reduce **8** employs **9** directors **10** earns

Business know-how

1 Get students to discuss the question. Round up at class level and make notes on the board.

2 Ask students to read the tips and compare them with the ideas on the board. Ask them to tell you which tips they find most helpful.

3 Get students to read the job advert and make a note of the skills and qualities which they already have for the job. Ask students to prepare their answers to the questions: *Why do you want this job? What can you bring to this job? What are your strengths? What's your biggest weakness? What is the greatest achievement in your last job?*

4 Brainstorm with the students some ideas about what BPQ could be like: *What sort of company is it? How big is it? When was it established? What sort of fashion does it sell?* etc. Make notes on the board. Then in pairs get students to interview each other using the questions as guidelines. Encourage them to use the tips from *Business know-how.* Ask some stronger pairs to perform their interviews in front of the class.

Writing

Ask students to read the advert again and write a letter of application. They should use the guidelines to help them structure the letter. If they haven't already done it, go to *Writing bank*, Letters 2, page 59. If they have done it, remind them to follow the advice on that page.

➕ Additional activity
(weaker students)
Ask students to take a couple of minutes to re-read the article then ask them to close their books. Dictate these numbers and dates:
1982 1990 2003
25% 39%
$4 million $35 million
two thirds 6–8 2,500 6

➕ Additional activity
(weaker students)
Ask students to read the advert and answer these questions:
1 *What sort of company is it?*
2 *What post are they looking to fill?*
3 *What sort of personality are they looking for?*
4 *What are the main duties?*
5 *What are the main soft skills they would like?*

➕ Writing bank
CV1 and CV2
Go to pp.63 and 64 Student's Book.

➕ Photocopiable activity CV
Go to p.101 Teacher's Resource Book.

Instructions for photocopiable activities

1 First day

1 Ask students to work in pairs and discuss the questions.

2 Get students to read the blogs and discuss the questions.

> 🔑 **good experiences** meeting co-workers, nice co-workers, new PC
> **bad experiences** not remembering names and information, manager and colleagues too busy, problem with PC, arrived late

3 In groups get students to write their top ten tips.

4 Students exchange their ideas and discuss the advice.

2 Business activities

1 Get students to work in groups and make a list. Round up at class level.

2 Get students to read the definitions and classify the industries in their lists.

3 Get students to brainstorm their ideas in pairs and round up at class level.

4 Get student to discuss their ideas in groups and then discuss at class level.

3 Consumer profiles

1 Get students to discuss their ideas in pairs. Round up at class level.

2 Get students to read the text and answer the question.

> 🔑 no product can be suitable for everyone, by dividing the market into groups you can identify their needs and aim your product at them

3 Get students to discuss their ideas in pairs and round up at class level.

4 Get students to do the matching exercise and compare with their answers for exercise 3.

> 🔑 a status in family   b disposable income
> c age   d gender   e location   f family size
> g culture and lifestyle   h marital status

5 Get students to discuss the products and services in groups.

4 Keep talking

Cut up enough cards for the groups in your class. Divide the class into groups and distribute the cards. The aim of the activity is to speak for as long as possible on each subject.

5 Contemporary trends

1 & 2 Introduce the aim of the activity to the students. Divide the class into groups and ask them to choose an issue. Ask the individuals in the group to do activity 2 on their own.

3 Get students to compare their ideas in groups. Encourage them to use future forms.

4 If time, get students to repeat the exercise with another topic.

6 Culture shock

1 Get students to do the exercise.

2 Ask students to discuss their reactions in pairs.

3 Get students to compare the information with their own culture. Round up at class level.

4 Students can write a guide in class in pairs or for homework.

7 Ethical consumers

1 Ask students to read the article and answer the question.

2 Ask students to work in pairs and read the extracts. They should discuss the information in relation to the questions. Round up ideas at class level.

3 Ask students to do the questionnaire in pairs and discuss their answers. They can write a paragraph about their consumer habits for homework.

8 Diversity and discrimination

1 Ask students to work in groups and think of different kinds of discrimination. Round up ideas at class level.

2 Ask students to read the article and match the categories with the definitions.

> 🔑 1 B   2 A   3 C

3 Ask students to read the examples and decide which types of discrimination they show.

> 🔑 a 1   b 2   c 3   d 2   e 1   f 3   g 2

4 Ask students to research the organizations on the Internet and write a paragraph about each one.

9 A new brand

1 Ask students to work in groups and choose a product.

2 Get students to invent a name. Encourage them to be creative with English and use dictionaries to do the exercise.

3 Get students to design a logo. The most artistic member of the group can do a finished version of the logo.

4 Students should think of the core values for their brand. Refer them back to the lesson on core values for ideas.

5 Brainstorm slogans at class level. Then get students to think of a slogan for their product.

6 If possible, get students to do a poster about their product and put the products on the walls. Students can then go round and choose the ones they like best.

10 Work spaces

1 Ask students to work in pairs and discuss the work spaces guessing what the people who use them are like.

2 Ask students to discuss the questions in pairs.

3 Get students to make notes of their ideal work space individually.

4 Ask students to discuss their ideal work spaces in pairs. Round up at class level.

11 Difficult conversations

Divide the class into Student As and Student Bs. Give out the role cards and give students time to understand their roles. They should brainstorm the language they are going to use. Then put the students in pairs (A and B) and ask them to do the role play. Round up at class level and give students feedback on their performance.

12 Presentations – FAQs

1 Ask students to discuss the questions in pairs. Round up at class level.

2 Ask students to match the questions and answers.

> **O⚷** A 6   B 1   C 3   D 5

3 Ask students to discuss the advice in groups. Then round up at class level.

13 Multinationals

1 Ask students to discuss the multinationals in groups. Round up at class level.

> **O⚷ Some information**
> **Walmart** (US) owns Asda supermarkets, Sam's Club warehouses
> **Toyota** (Japan) owns Lexus Scion Daihatsu (51.2%)
> **Microsoft** (US) owns assets MSNBC cable network, MSN Internet portal, etc.
> **Nokia** (Finland) merged with Siemens
> **Coca-Cola** (US) brands include Fanta and Sprite, sells Dr Pepper and Schweppes
> **Shell** (Netherlands) involved in exploration, gas and power, chemicals and shipping
> **Nestlé** (Switzerland) owns Findus, San Pellegrino water, etc.
> **McDonald's** (US) owns Donatos pizza, has a minority stake in Prêt à Manger

2 Ask students to make notes in pairs about the advantages and disadvantages of multinationals. Round up at class level.

3 Ask students to read the article and identify any of their ideas from exercises 1 and 2.

4 Get students to discuss the opinions in groups. They can write a paragraph about the opinion they feel most strongly about.

14 Managing a budget

1 Ask students to read the text in pairs and think of advice to give students. Round up at class level.

2 Get students to read the article and tick the advice they thought of.

3 Get students to discuss the questions in groups. Round up at class level.

15 CVs

1 Ask students to read the CV on their own and decide what is wrong with it.

> **O⚷ Possible answers**
> **layout** no use of bold in headings, the examples of work experience should start with the most recent work, bullet points should be used for information, etc.
> **contents** no phone or email address, 'I' shouldn't be used in *Profile*, inappropriate information in *Major achievements*, too many sports listed under *Experience*, no dates under *Education*, inappropriate *References* line, etc.
> **grammar and spelling** studnets, Admininstrative, 'I have done general office work', eccellent, etc.

2 Get students to compare their answers.

1 Grammar test

1 Read about Krystyna and underline the correct form of the verbs.

> **Case studies**
>
> **FAQ**
>
> **Contact us**
>
> **My working environment:** Krystyna Dabrowski
>
> **Placement:** I'm a student and I ¹ *do / 'm doing* a course in business studies and public relations. At the moment I ² *finish / 'm finishing* an 8-week internship in a marketing department.
>
> **Hours:** Normally I ³ *start / 'm starting* at 9 and ⁴ *finish / finishing* at 5.30. However, we're incredibly busy at the moment so I ⁵ *work / 'm working* late most evenings. But that's OK. The work is interesting so time ⁶ *passes / is passing* very quickly.
>
> **Activities:** I ⁷ *deal / 'm dealing* with lots of emails and phone calls. I ⁸ *liaise / 'm liaising* with journalists and our PR agency. At the moment I ⁹ *prepare / 'm preparing* next year's catalogue. We ¹⁰ *have / are having* a tight deadline so I ¹¹ *put in / 'm putting in* a lot of extra hours.
>
> **Likes and dislikes:** It's a friendly working environment and I ¹² *love / 'm loving* the interaction with people. That's definitely the best thing.

2 Complete the dialogues with the Present Simple or the Present Continuous form of the verbs in brackets.

1 **A** *Are you* (you, be) busy at the moment?

 B Yes, I *am* (be), actually. I *'m trying* (try) to finish a presentation for tomorrow.

2 **A** What time _____ Joseph usually _____ (get) to the office?

 B He normally _____ (arrive) before nine, but he _____ (have) problems with the traffic this morning.

3 **A** _____ the coffee machine _____ (work) today?

 B I _____ (not know). I always _____ (make) my own drinks.

4 **A** Where _____ you _____ (live) at the moment?

 B I _____ (rent) a small flat in the centre, but I _____ (hope) to find something a bit cheaper nearer the office.

5 **A** What _____ Farid and Emily _____ (do)?

 B They _____ (make) a conference call to the Tokyo office.

6 **A** What _____ Tina _____ (think) about her new manager?

 B Well, she _____ (say) she likes him, but I _____ (not believe) her!

3 Look at the Present Simple and Present Continuous verbs. Tick (✔) the correct ones, cross (✗) the wrong ones, and write the correct form of the verbs.

1 ☒ My department <u>is</u> always <u>trying</u> *tries* to stick to deadlines.

2 ☐ Lucinda<u>'s talking</u> to some new clients at the moment.

3 ☐ <u>Are</u> you <u>wanting</u> to finish work on time today?

4 ☐ Akiko <u>aims</u> to finish a report by the end of the day.

5 ☐ This week we<u>'re</u> mainly <u>preparing</u> a mailshot.

6 ☐ Lucas <u>has</u> a meeting with his manager at 3.30 today.

7 ☐ In my office most people <u>are</u> usually <u>eating</u> their lunches at their desks.

8 ☐ What <u>are</u> you <u>working</u> on at the moment?

1 First day

1 Work in pairs. What can go wrong on the first day in a new job?
- *You arrive late.*
- *You can't remember everybody's name.*

2 Read the blogs and answer the questions.
1. What were their good and bad experiences?
2. Who do you think had the best / worst days? Why?

My first day

My manager took me round the department and introduced me to everyone. It was great to meet all my co-workers but I couldn't remember any of their names afterwards! Then I had a tour of the building – it's huge. My feet were aching at the end of the day! People gave me a lot of information – I couldn't remember much of that, either. But everyone seemed really enthusiastic and friendly. I'm looking forward to my second day.

Katrina

Today was my first day in my new job, and it was pretty awful. My manager was tied up in meetings most of the day – he was apologetic, but he didn't have time to talk to me and tell me what I should do. My colleagues seemed too busy to talk much.
I tried to smile at everyone and look friendly but I think I seemed a bit mad! I had real problems with my PC, too. I had to keep phoning IT and I'm sure they got fed up with me. Hope tomorrow's better!

Alberto

I got a laptop, a desk next to a window ☺, and a phone. I spent most of the morning installing software and reading some intranet stuff. I went with a couple of co-workers to the staff restaurant. The food wasn't great but they were both nice. We're going out for a drink at the end of the week.

Matt

The day started badly ☹. I arrived late (my train was cancelled!). Very embarrassing! My first meeting was with Human Resources. They gave me lots of background information on the company, details of the pension scheme (I'm only 20!), and things like that. I didn't get to my office before 11. It's open plan – and noisy! There's a lot of positive energy. I've got a great PC – silver, shiny and with a 15-inch screen. I love it ☺.

Lucia

3 Work in groups. Write your top ten tips for people starting a new job.

Ten tips for starting a new job
1. *Get up early so you can arrive on time.*
2. *Take some cash in case you have to buy lunch.*
3. _____
4. _____
5. _____
6. _____
7. _____
8. _____
9. _____
10. _____

4 Exchange your list with another group. Who gave the best / clearest / most useful / most unusual advice?

2 Grammar test

1 Complete the texts with the Past Simple or the Past Continuous form of the verbs in brackets.

1 I [1] _was attending_ (attend) a sales conference when I [2] _____ (go) to a fascinating session about 'wants and needs'. I [3] _____ (talk) to the speaker afterwards. While we [4] _____ (chat) I realised that she was in the same class as me at school!

2 After Miu [5] _____ (graduate) from university, she [6] _____ (take) a gap year. She [7] _____ (travel) and [8] _____ (do) temp work in several countries, including South Africa and Australia. She [9] _____ (work) for an import export company in Sydney when she [10] _____ (decide) she [11] _____ (want) to stay there permanently.

3 It was half past three and Javier [12] _____ (feel) tired. So he [13] _____ (get up) from his desk and [14] _____ (start) moving his arms and legs. He [15] _____ (stretch) from side to side when he [16] _____ (hear) a cough behind him. He [17] _____ (turn) and [18] _____ (see) his boss with a client.

4 Laura [19] _____ (do) an internship with a software developer and Elena [20] _____ (finish) her final year at business school when they [21] _____ (set up) their own online company.

2 Complete the sentences with *when* or *while*. Sometimes either word may be possible.

1 Nobody was talking _when_ I walked into the office.

2 Lucas visited several new clients _____ he was staying in London.

3 Tereza was driving to the factory of a new supplier _____ she realized she was lost.

4 He downloaded a computer virus _____ he was surfing the Net at work.

5 They were discussing the recent sales figures _____ Mr Abaza announced that the whole sales team was going to receive a bonus.

6 _____ we were waiting to start the meeting, I discovered that I didn't have the right documents with me.

3 Complete the dialogues with the correct form of the verbs in the boxes and the words in brackets. Use short forms.

| decide be (×2) accept ~~not come~~ go (×2) see talk (×2) seem |

A Why [1] _didn't you come_ (you) to the planning meeting this morning?

B Oh, I [2] _____ a bit busy.

A When I [3] _____ to the meeting I [4] _____ you were on the phone.

B That's right. It [5] _____ a customer.

A You [6] _____ very happy.

B Did I?

A Come on, tell me. Who [7] _____ (you) to really?

B OK, if you promise not to tell anyone. I [8] _____ to the Head of Human Resources at Reflex. I [9] _____ for an interview there last week, and they've offered me a job!

A [10] _____ (you) it?

B Yes, and that's why I [11] _____ not to go to the meeting.

A Well, that's amazing. Congratulations!

2 Business activities

1 Work in groups. Make a list of the ten main industries and businesses in your country.

financial services
coal mining
tourism

2 Read the following definitions, then classify your ideas from exercise 1 as *primary*, *secondary* or *tertiary*.

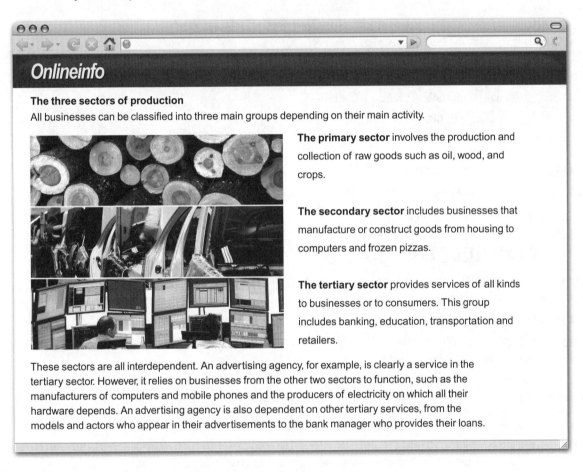

Onlineinfo

The three sectors of production

All businesses can be classified into three main groups depending on their main activity.

The primary sector involves the production and collection of raw goods such as oil, wood, and crops.

The secondary sector includes businesses that manufacture or construct goods from housing to computers and frozen pizzas.

The tertiary sector provides services of all kinds to businesses or to consumers. This group includes banking, education, transportation and retailers.

These sectors are all interdependent. An advertising agency, for example, is clearly a service in the tertiary sector. However, it relies on businesses from the other two sectors to function, such as the manufacturers of computers and mobile phones and the producers of electricity on which all their hardware depends. An advertising agency is also dependent on other tertiary services, from the models and actors who appear in their advertisements to the bank manager who provides their loans.

3 Work in pairs. Think of one of your favourite DVDs. Which business activities were involved in its production? Brainstorm your ideas, then label them P (Primary), S (Secondary) or T (Tertiary).

filming and recording (S)
transporting DVDs to warehouse (T)
felling of trees for wood pulp (P)

4 Work in groups. Discuss the following questions.

- What is happening to the primary, secondary and tertiary sectors in your country? Are they growing or declining? Why?
- What is happening to the following business activities in your country or region?

agriculture	*clothes manufacturing*	*financial services*
mining	**education**	**car manufacturing**

3 Grammar test

1 Complete the dialogues with the Present Perfect Simple or Present Perfect Continuous form of the verbs in brackets.

A How long [1] *have you been working* (work) in this department now?

B Just over three months.

A [2] _____ (go) on an induction course yet?

B No, I [3] _____ .

....

A [4] _____ (you, see) Andy? He looks terrible. His eyes are all red. Has he [5] _____ (cry)?

B No, he [6] _____ (just, get back) from Los Angeles. He's suffering from jet lag!

....

A Who [7] _____ (leave) their mobile phone on the table?

B I don't know. I [8] _____ (sit) here all afternoon and this is the first time I [9] _____ (notice) it.

....

A How are you going to market the new product?

B Well, we [10] _____ (talk) about it for hours but we still [11] _____ (not decide).

2 Match the questions (1–6) and the answers (a–f).

> ## STAFF QUESTIONNAIRE
>
> 1 Have you spoken to any customers today? _a_
> 2 What have you been doing this morning? ____
> 3 Have you ever given a presentation? ____
> 4 Have you had your staff appraisal yet? ____
> 5 Have you done any overtime this month? ____
> 6 Have you ever surfed the Net during office hours? ____

a I *have talked* (talk) to two or three. But they were only simple enquiries so they didn't take long.

b No, not yet. I _____ (speak) to my manager and we _____ (try) to fix a date. But this is a very busy time of year.

c Well, I _____ (write) about 20 emails. And I _____ (work) on a market research report. I still _____ (not finish) that.

d Yes, I think I _____ (do) about three or four hours.

e Yes, I _____ . In fact, I _____ (do) it for the last hour. I'm looking for a flight to Lisbon next week. But don't worry. It's a work trip!

f No, I _____ . But for the past few days I _____ (prepare) a talk I have to give next week. My manager's going to be there and I'm a bit nervous.

3 Now complete the answers with the Present Perfect Simple or Continuous form of the verbs in brackets. Use the Continuous form where possible.

4 In your notebook write sentences about you.

- Write about three things that you have been doing recently.
- Write about three things that you have done this year.

3 Consumer profiles

1 Work in pairs. What factors affect the way people spend their money? Note your ideas.

age
where you live
the size of families

2 Read the text and answer the question.
Why is it important for businesses to divide consumers into different segments?

MARKET SEGMENTS

Businesses want to capture as much of the market as possible – but there are problems. Each company faces considerable competition from other businesses, and no company can produce a product that will be suitable for everybody.

So companies try to produce market-orientated products – products that match the needs, wants, and expectations of specific segments or sections of the market. A market segment is a large group of possible customers who are similar in age, income, where they live, etc. Marketing theory is based on the simple idea that people who are similar will spend their money in similar ways. If you want to promote and sell your products, first identify your customer!

3 Work in pairs. How do the following factors affect the way people spend their money? Note your ideas.

age	gender	disposable income	family size
status in family	culture & lifestyle	location	marital status

4 Match the following notes with the headings above. Did you make any of the same points?

a the 'head' of the family will make key decisions about which electricity supplier to use, when and where to buy groceries, etc.

b stores offering luxury products target affluent customers, other retail stores concentrate on people with tight budgets

c *many older people want to feel young and keep fit – and if they have company pensions, they have the money to spend on this*

d *this is important for companies producing clothes, toiletries, cosmetics, and many magazines*

e *regions within countries and different countries have different needs*

f larger families often have less time and less money to spend

g *this is linked to people's religion, dietary habits, language, and customs*

h a young single person will have different priorities to a married couple with two children

5 Work in groups. Imagine you work in a marketing department. Which market segments would you target for the following products and services?

home insurance	a new, smaller MP3	a Mediterranean cruise
anti-wrinkle face cream	fun, cheap jewellery	a private pension scheme

4 Grammar test

1 Complete the sentences for the following situations with *should have* or *shouldn't have* and the correct form of the verb.

1 Claudia didn't check the estimated costs. Her project went seriously over budget.

Claudia *should have checked* the estimated costs.

2 Michael criticized his secretary in front of other members of staff. They were very embarrassed.

Michael _____ his secretary in front of other members of staff.

3 Laurence didn't attend the review meeting. Later she was reprimanded by her manager.

Laurence _____ the review meeting.

4 Jacek used Roz's computer without asking her.

Jacek _____ Roz's computer without asking her.

5 Rachel and Nicole chatted throughout the team meeting. They annoyed their colleagues.

Rachel and Nicole _____ throughout the meeting.

6 Sara didn't take notes during the presentation. It caused problems later.

Sara _____ notes during the presentation.

2 Read the chatroom messages and underline the correct form of the verbs.

| **Katalin** |
| I can't stand the place where I work. I [1] *should have spoken* / *will have to speak* to Human Resources months ago when I was first unhappy. Now I think I [2] *had to* / *'ll have to* apply for another job. |

| **Owen** |
| In my last job, the office was really relaxed. We [3] *didn't have to* / *had to* wear smart clothes. |

| **Jade** |
| My manager expected me to work longer hours than my colleagues. I always [4] *should have* / *had to* take work home and work at weekends. |

| **Sandro** |
| My last boss believed very strongly in personal development. We [5] *should have gone* / *had to go* on lots of teambuilding and training courses. It was quite inspirational. |

| **Isabel** |
| My last boss was great. I [6] *didn't have to* / *will have to* start before 10 or work late. I [7] *had to* / *shouldn't have* changed my job. I'll never have another boss like him! |

3 Answer the questions about you.

1 What did you have to do last week?

_____

2 What should you have done last week?

_____

3 What will you have to do next week?

_____

4 Keep talking

Play this game in groups of three or four students.

Take it in turns to pick a card.
Talk about the topic for as long as possible.
The person who can talk for the longest is the winner.

a bad leader	**my ideal job**	**how to get energized at work**
my favourite magazine	**what I'm reading**	**a good leader**
how to avoid time-wasting	**the last thing I bought**	**mobile phone etiquette**
in five years' time	**tips for learning English**	**my favourite film**

5 Grammar test

1 Complete the dialogues with *will* or *going to* and the phrases from the box.

apply for it	get you	be free	do it	leave
ask for a promotion	send it again	~~type them up~~		

1 **A** Have you written up the minutes from the last meeting?
  B Sorry! I forgot all about it. I *'ll type them up* as soon as I can.

2 **A** Where's Tanya?
  B She's in a meeting. I don't think she _____ for a couple of hours.

3 **A** Did you get my email?
  B Yes, but I can't open the attachment.
  A OK, I _____.

4 **A** Are you interested in the International Exhibition Organizer job?
  B Yes, I am. I _____. In fact, I'm updating my CV at the moment!

5 **A** Andrew looks nervous.
  B Yeah, well, he's decided to talk to his manager. He _____.

6 **A** What's the matter?
  B I'm exhausted.
  A OK, I _____ a double espresso.

7 **A** Do you want me to read your presentation?
  B That's OK. I spoke to Magdalena earlier. She _____.

8 **A** Have you heard the news? The managing director _____.
  B When?
  A Next month, apparently.

2 Look at the following sentences. Tick (✔) the correct ones, cross (✘) the wrong ones, and correct them.

1 ☐ Liam <u>isn't going to come</u> to the three o'clock meeting. He has other commitments.

2 ☐ The company's new website is going to go online tomorrow. We hope it <u>is having</u> a great impact.

3 ☐ Sandro can't work late this evening. He <u>will meet</u> a former colleague at half past six.

4 ☐ 'How does this programme work?' 'Don't worry, I <u>explain</u>.'

5 ☐ When <u>are</u> you <u>knowing</u> the sales figures?

6 ☐ 'Would you like a drink?' 'I<u>'m going to have</u> a fresh orange juice, please.'

3 Complete the sentences with *will have to* or *will be able to* and the following verbs. They may be positive or negative.

access	work	take on	meet	~~protect~~	start

1 We *will have to protect* our computer system against hackers.

2 Digital communication means that more people _____ from home.

3 My computer has just crashed. I _____ that presentation all over again.

4 The IT department is carrying out important work over the weekend so staff _____ their email accounts.

5 I'm free on Thursday so I _____ you for lunch.

6 If the online business continues to grow, they _____ more staff.

4 In your notebook write sentences about you. What will you have to do if you want to …?
  • improve your English   • find a good job   • have a successful year

5 Contemporary trends

In this activity you are going to examine different issues that have an impact on business and our lives.

1 Work in groups of four. Choose one of the issues below to examine.

A Working from home

B Cheap air travel

C Banning cars from city centres

D The Internet

2 Work on your own and consider the following questions.

What impact is the issue you have chosen having on people's lives?
What impact will it have in the coming ten years?

Think about the following areas:
- social
- economic
- environmental
- personal

Make a note of your ideas in the table below.

Positive	Negative

3 Work in your groups and discuss your ideas. Use the Expressions from page 32 of the Student's Book.

4 In your groups, choose another topic and do the exercise again.

6 Grammar test

1 Complete the sentences with *must* or *can't* and the verbs from the box.

| belong   feel   enjoy   come   want   know   ~~speak~~   have   be (×2) |

1 Shika has worked in Paris for five years so she *must speak* fluent French.
2 Gilberto hasn't updated his CV so he _____ ready to apply for the job.
3 You don't even go to foreign restaurants. You _____ to work abroad.
4 Olivia seems to get on with everybody. She _____ quite an extrovert.
5 Ethan calls home from Japan every week. I think he _____ homesick.
6 This old mobile _____ to Sophie. She only buys the latest models.
7 Agnieszka did an internship with a finance company so she _____ about hedge funds.
8 Carlo doesn't understand Italian so he _____ from Italy.
9 Leon always looks enthusiastic. He _____ working here.
10 Sameera looks very happy. She _____ a new job.

2 Re-write the sentences using *must, can't* or *may / could*.

1 You don't think you will go to the meeting. You aren't sure.
   I may not go to the meeting.
2 Tim is late for work. You are sure he is caught in a traffic jam.
   Tim must be caught in a traffic jam.
3 The sales figures seem too low. You are sure they aren't right.

   _____

4 Christopher is very quiet today. It is possible he is depressed.

   _____

5 Simona looks very tired. You are sure she is working too much.

   _____

6 You have received no phone calls. You are sure there is a fault on the line.

   _____

7 Alex is thinking about taking a gap year. He isn't sure.

   _____

8 You can hear a mobile phone. You are sure it isn't yours.

   _____

3 Underline the correct modal verbs to complete the sentences.

1 **A** Have you seen David today?
   B No, I haven't. I think he *might* / *must* be working at home. I'm not sure.
2 **A** Who's that guy talking to Melissa?
   B I think it's Harry's new PA.
   A That *can't* / *must* be him. He's too old. Harry's new PA is in his twenties.
3 **A** I think we *could* / *can't* meet our targets for this month.
   B Really?
   A Yes, the figures are looking much better.
4 **A** My colleague Karen has decided to take a job in Canada.
   B You *might* / *must* be very upset. Everyone really likes her, don't they?
5 **A** Did you know that Alex writes a work blog?
   B He *could* / *can't* have enough work to do!

6 Culture shock

1 How much do you know about British behaviour and gestures? Read the article.

Underline the information you know.
Circle the information you find surprising.

Everything you wanted to know about the British but were afraid to ask

- When paying a cashier, people always place the money in the cashier's hand.
- A 'V' sign made with the fingers with the palm towards the viewer means 'victory' or 'peace'.
- A 'V' sign made with the back of the hand towards the viewer is very offensive.
- If British people accidentally touch someone they usually say 'excuse me' or 'sorry'.
- Queueing is normal when there is a demand for an item. This doesn't happen in pubs. However, it's rude to accept service from a barperson before someone who has been waiting longer.
- It is normal in Britain to pack your own groceries at a supermarket check-out. Sometimes a cashier will offer to help.
- When people go to a pub with friends or colleagues, it is normal to take turns in buying drinks for everyone. This is called 'buying a round'.
- Attracting the attention of a shop worker or a waiter with gestures (especially by snapping the fingers) is rude.
- However, you can ask the waiter to bring the bill by making a writing gesture with one hand (as a pen) on the other hand (as paper).
- When invited round for dinner, it is expected that the guests will bring a bottle of wine or a gift such as flowers or chocolates.
- Kissing or hugging after a first introduction is very unusual.

- On escalators at train stations, people stand on the right and overtake on the left.
- However, they walk on the left-hand side in corridors or walkways.
- The British don't walk slowly in groups on the pavement.
- They usually add a tip of 10% to the bill in restaurants unless a service charge has already been included.
- They don't eat chips (French fries) with their fingers in restaurants or at people's homes. Fingers are often used for eating meat on the bone such as chicken.

2 Work in pairs. Compare your responses to the text.

3 Work in pairs. Read the article again and compare the behaviour in the UK to what you do in your own culture.

4 Write a guide for visitors to your country on acceptable behaviour and gestures.

7 Grammar test

1 Complete the article with the passive form of the verbs in the box.

suspend	hold	claim	report	arrest
study	invest	discover	force	~~believe~~

The collapse of Parmalat

After the financial scandals at Enron and WorldCom, it ¹ *was believed* that no similar fraud could happen in Europe. Then came the collapse of Parmalat. When Parmalat failed to make a $185 million bond payment in November 2003, its accounts ² _____ by auditors and banks. It ³ _____ that 38% of Parmalat's assets ⁴ _____ in a Bank of America account in the Cayman Islands. But on 19 December, it ⁵ _____ by the Bank of America that no such account existed. In the subsequent investigation, it ⁶ _____ that assets ⁷ _____ to offset up to $16.2 billion in liabilities and falsified accounts. The company ⁸ _____ into bankruptcy on 27 December. Trading in Parmalat shares ⁹ _____ on the same day. The founder of Parmalat, Calisto Tanzi, Chief Financial Officer, Fausto Tonna, and 18 other people ¹⁰ _____ .

2 Complete the sentences using the correct form of the passive.

1 The Fairtrade minimum price *is calculated* (calculate) to cover the costs of sustainable production and a sustainable livelihood.

2 The repairs _____ (complete) by the beginning of next week.

3 _____ (children, exploit) in the production of these goods?

4 Our working practices _____ (reviewed) at the moment.

5 The company _____ (found) in the early 1960s.

6 Since 1998, our efforts to use Fairtrade products _____ (increase).

7 The Internet _____ (use) by campaigners to put pressure on companies they don't approve of.

8 In the future, more locally-sourced food _____ (consume).

3 Make the active sentences passive. Use a phrase with *by*.

1 One of my colleagues will place an order later today.

   An order will be placed by one of my colleagues later today.

2 A large audience was listening to her presentation.

   Her presentation _____

3 Cafédirect is giving ethical investors the opportunity to buy shares in its company.

   Ethical investors _____

4 My manager must write the report.

   The report _____

5 The company might buy Fairtrade products later this year.

   Fairtrade products _____

6 Markus should have given a decision.

   A decision _____

7 Ethical consumers

1 Read the paragraph and answer the question. Why do you think there is a difference between what consumers believe and their spending habits?

An increasing number of people consider themselves ethical consumers. They actively choose to buy goods or services that are produced ethically – without harming or exploiting humans, animals, or the natural environment. In practice, however, while an increasing number of British consumers say they care about a company's record on social responsibility, ethical products only make up about 4% of total consumer spending.

2 Work in pairs. Read the extracts from a recent report and discuss the following points.
- Do you find any of the statistics surprising?
- Compare the statistics with attitudes in your country.

We asked 2,000 people about their attitudes to business and ethical consumerism. This is what we found:

Only **4%** strongly believe that companies behave ethically.

16% boycotted products for ethical reasons.

About **a quarter** bought a product because it was linked to a charity.

93% believe that companies should be responsible for improving the impact of their products and services on society.

Nearly **40%** have made **5 or more** ethical purchases in the last year.

Recycling is the most common 'ethical' activity (**77%**), followed by giving to charity (**70%**).

Over **90%** of employees believe their employer's policy on social responsibility is important.

Over **80%** take into account a company's social responsibility when they make a purchase.

Over **80%** of employees think their employer is socially responsible.

2% bought a RED product* last year.

*RED products are sold to raise money for women and children affected by AIDS in Africa

3 Work in pairs. Do you think you are an ethical consumer? Discuss the following questions, giving personal examples.

The ethical consumer
questionnaire

- Do you regularly recycle domestic waste (paper, glass, etc.)?
- Do you support local shops and suppliers?
- Do you ever recommend companies for their responsible reputation?
- Do you choose products or services because of a company's responsible reputation?
- Do you avoid products or services because of a company's reputation?
- Do you choose products mainly for ethical reasons?
- Do you actively look for information about a company's behaviour or policies?
- Do you feel guilty when you make an unethical purchase?
- Do you ever actively campaign about environmental or social issues?

8 Grammar test

1 Match the beginnings and ends of the sentences.

1 If companies employ more diverse workforces,   a you wouldn't like it.

2 If they introduce the new pay structure,   b it risks being shut down.

3 If we don't go online soon,   c we'll lose our market share.

4 If employees harass their colleagues,   d there would be less inequality in the workplace.

5 If more women were employed full time,   e diversity schemes won't work.

6 If managers don't genuinely care,   f their productivity increases.

7 If you had to do my job,   g we'll be better off.

8 If a Norwegian company has fewer than 40% women directors,   h they will be disciplined.

2 Complete the sentences using the first conditional. Use short forms.

1 Even if they _offer_ (offer) me the job, I _won't_ (not accept) it. I really didn't like the interview at all.

2 If I _____ (get) a salary increase, I _____ (take) a holiday. I'm not sure yet.

3 I think they _____ (be) disappointed if we _____ (not give) them a decision this afternoon.

4 If I _____ (see) Hoshi, I _____ (definitely, tell) him what happened.

5 I _____ (not, drive) my own car even if they _____ (pay) for the petrol. It's much easier by train.

6 What _____ (she, do) if she _____ (not, get) the qualification?

7 I'm sure my performance _____ (improve) if I _____ (go) on this course.

8 If we _____ (be able to) prove the company is responsible, they _____ (pay) damages.

3 Offer advice to colleagues for the following situations.

1 I have to produce spreadsheets and use a computer the whole time and I'm not very good at it.
   If I were you, _____

2 I have to entertain three British visitors to our company and I don't know what to do.
   _____

3 I have to give a presentation at a conference and I'm really nervous about it.
   _____

4 I have lots of things to do and I don't know where to begin.
   _____

5 My boss is always criticizing me and I don't know what I should do.
   _____

4 What would you do if you ...

1 lost your passport in a foreign country?
   _____

2 were going to be late for a job interview?
   _____

3 left your mobile phone in a taxi?
   _____

4 saw a colleague stealing office stationery?
   _____

8 Diversity and discrimination

1 Work in groups. What kinds of discrimination can take place inside an organization? Note your ideas and give examples.

Age
- *an older employee is never invited to social events by younger colleagues*
- *a company puts an age limit in a job advertisement*
- *older employees are not promoted*

2 Read the article, then match the categories with the definitions below.

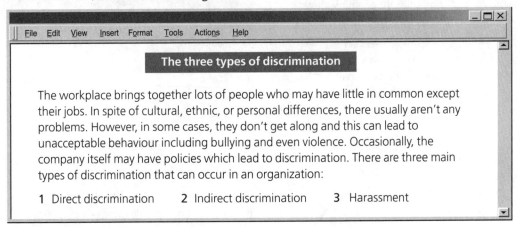

File   Edit   View   Insert   Format   Tools   Actions   Help

The three types of discrimination

The workplace brings together lots of people who may have little in common except their jobs. In spite of cultural, ethnic, or personal differences, there usually aren't any problems. However, in some cases, they don't get along and this can lead to unacceptable behaviour including bullying and even violence. Occasionally, the company itself may have policies which lead to discrimination. There are three main types of discrimination that can occur in an organization:

1 Direct discrimination   2 Indirect discrimination   3 Harassment

A Applying a condition or practice that makes it more difficult for certain groups inside an organization to get on.

_____

B Treating people differently on the basis of their sexual orientation, religion, ethnic background, gender, etc.

_____

C Behaviour that creates a hostile, offensive, or unpleasant environment.

_____

3 Decide if these examples of discrimination are Direct (1), Indirect (2), or Harassment (3).
a ☐1☐ A job advertisement says 'no disabled people need apply'.
b ☐ People who are different (e.g. for sexual orientation, religion) are denied their rights or are never offered jobs.
c ☐ Making sexual comments about a colleague in his/her presence.
d ☐ Women are only given certain jobs while men take the others.
e ☐ People with disabilities are automatically rejected from certain jobs.
f ☐ Making jokes about particular groups of people.
g ☐ A particular ethnic group tend to be given certain jobs.

4 Use the Internet to find out about the following organizations. Then find out if there are similar organizations in your own country.
- *Kick racism out of football*
- *The Commission for Racial Equality*
- *Equal Opportunities Commission*

9 Grammar test

1 Underline the correct tense of the verb to complete the sentences.

1 They only <u>launched</u> / had launched the new brand after they established / <u>had established</u> its core values and they conducted / <u>had conducted</u> extensive research.

2 When the Marketing manager got / had got to the meeting, we already discussed / had already discussed the main points on the agenda.

3 Before Levi Strauss & Co. decided / had decided to concentrate on manufacturing jeans, it mainly focused / had mainly focused on dry goods wholesaling.

4 Although they sponsored / had sponsored several major sporting events, research revealed / had revealed only a small increase in their brand recognition.

5 When we met / had met for the brainstorming session, Alain revealed / had revealed that he thought of / had thought of a new slogan.

6 Rudolph Dassler already lauched / had already launched the Puma brand of trainers in 1948, when his brother Adi Dassler founded / had founded Adidas in 1949.

7 We decided / had decided that we needed to have another meeting after we rejected / had rejected all of the possible brand names.

8 We got / had got to the conference after the opening session started / had started.

2 Match the beginnings and ends of the sentences. Change one verb in each sentence to the Past Perfect Simple.

1 I couldn't find my way to their office because
2 I felt really stressed because
3 I didn't do very well at the interview because
4 I didn't go to the meeting because
5 I wasn't very happy with Simon because
6 I felt incredibly hungry during the meeting because
7 I tried the new product because
8 I couldn't do any research all day because

a I was very impressed by the packaging.
b he used my laptop without asking me first.
c I failed to meet an important deadline.
d the server went down.
e I missed my breakfast.
f I ~~left~~ *had left* the directions on my desk.
g I fixed another appointment for the same time.
h I wasn't able to get to sleep the night before.

3 Use the Past Perfect to complete the sentences.

1 Mark said, 'Giacomo has been delayed at Rome Airport.'
Mark said that Giacomo <u>had been delayed at Rome Airport.</u>

2 Lisa said, 'I haven't attended an overseas trade fair before.'
Lisa said that she _____

3 Yesterday Luis said, 'I've always wanted to work abroad.'
Luis told me that he _____

4 Jacob said, 'I know your manager. I met her at a conference last year.'
Jacob said that he knew my manager because _____

5 Keiko said, 'Have you worked in Tokyo before?'
Keiko asked if I _____

6 Larry said, 'We can't start the meeting because Lauren has just gone out.'
Larry explained that we couldn't start the meeting because Lauren _____

_____

9 A new brand

In this activity you are going to create a new brand. You can either continue the work you started in the Project on page 70 of the Student's Book or start with a fresh idea.

1 Work in groups of four. Choose a product (e.g. an MP3 player, a mobile phone, a computer, etc.).

2 Invent a brand name. You can make up a new word or use existing words. Brainstorm as many ideas as you can before choosing.

> **✳ Tip**
> Use a dictionary.

3 Design a logo. This is a symbol, a word, or a short phrase which is designed in a special way.

> **✳ Tip**
> Think of successful logos. Why are they memorable? Are they simple or complex? Do they contain words or a symbol?

4 Decide on the five core values of your brand. How is your brand different from rival brands?

> **✳ Tip**
> Think of other brands. For example, the core values of Virgin are *good quality*, *excellent customer service*, *innovative*, *competitively challenging*, and *fun*.

5 Write a slogan.

> **✳ Tip**
> Note any slogans you can remember (e.g. Apple 'Think different', Sony 'Like no other', Motorola 'Hello Moto'). Are they memorable / successful? Why?

6 Look at the brand ideas of other groups and choose the most successful one. Why have you chosen it? Make notes.

Product:	
Brand name:	
Logo:	
Slogan:	
Core Values:	

10 Grammar test

1 Complete the sentences with *must / can't have* and the correct form of the verbs in the box.

| tidy ~~miss~~ talk exceed get go out work finish |

1 **A** Why hasn't Javier come to this meeting?

   B He *must have missed* your email.

2 Lucia isn't at her desk. She _____ for lunch.

3 Jake _____ in an open plan office before. He keeps complaining to his manager about the noise and distractions.

4 **A** Alex didn't leave the office until 11 o'clock last night. But he looks relaxed today.

   B He _____ his sales presentation.

5 Look at the state of Astrid's desk! It's such a mess. She _____ it in months.

6 Jerry is looking rather miserable today. He _____ his promotion.

7 **A** You _____ to Alicia at the conference. She wasn't there.

   B Really? Then who did I talk to?

8 Ramon _____ his sales target last year. He's just got a fabulous bonus.

2 Write two possible explanations for the following situations. Use *might have* and *could have*.

1 It's 10.30 and Julie has only just arrived at the office.

   She might have overslept. She could have lost her alarm clock.

2 Florian is usually very talkative. However, at today's meeting he was very quiet.

   _____

3 It's 4.30 and Jakub isn't at his desk.

   _____

4 Silvo can hardly stay awake at work.

   _____

5 Katie has spent the whole morning surfing the Net.

   _____

3 Read the following sentences then write explanations for the situations in exercise 2. Use *must have*.

1 Julie complained about the traffic.

   _____

2 Florian took some painkillers.

   _____

3 Jakub said that he was feeling very thirsty.

   _____

4 Silvio has been doing a lot of overtime.

   _____

5 Katie has applied for two jobs.

   _____

10 Work spaces

1 Work in pairs. Look at the work spaces and describe the kind of people who you think use them.

2 Work in pairs. Look at the photos and discuss:
- which one you like best (Why?)
- which one you like least (Why?)
- how these work spaces could be improved (make suggestions)

3 What is your ideal work space? Make notes.
- location and layout (open plan, shared office, hot desking, private office, at home, etc.)
- position (internal, by a window, ground floor, etc.)
- equipment and office furniture (laptop, wireless PC, mobile phone, MP3 player, filing cabinet, curved or straight desk, lighting, etc.)
- personal items (posters, post cards, mugs, flowers, etc.)

4 Discuss your ideas with a partner.

11 Grammar test

1 Match the beginnings and ends of these sentences.

1 If she had asked for help,
2 If he hadn't done the anger management course,
3 We wouldn't have made such good progress
4 If he had been better organized,
5 What would you have done
6 If he hadn't been so nervous,
7 There would have been a better atmosphere
8 Would she have finished in time

a if the plane had been delayed?
b he wouldn't have lost the files.
c if she had had better time management skills?
d we could have finished the job this morning.
e if she had tried to be a team member.
f he would have lost his temper.
g he would have made a better impression.
h if we hadn't invested in staff training.

2 Complete the third conditional sentences using the verbs in brackets.

1 I _would have called_ (call) you if I _had known_ (know) it was important.
2 What _____ (you, do) if she _____ (continue) to be uncooperative?
3 If the company _____ (be) more adaptable, this situation _____ (never, happen).
4 Would _____ (he, win) the contract if he _____ (be) more organized?
5 My communication skills _____ (not, develop) if I _____ (not, do) voluntary work after school.
6 If she _____ (meet) her deadlines, we _____ (not, upset) the client.
7 I _____ (go) to the presentation if you _____ (tell) me about it.
8 If the trains _____ (be) more reliable, I _____ (not, fly) to the conference.

3 Use the prompts to write third conditional sentences.

1 I couldn't attend the course. I had far too much work.
   I would have attended the course if I hadn't had far too much work.
2 There was a traffic jam. We didn't get to the meeting on time.
   _____
3 Jan didn't listen closely to the customer. He didn't get the order.
   _____
4 Michael failed the exam. He didn't get the job as a translator.
   _____
5 Karen didn't get the job. She doesn't have good communication skills.
   _____
6 Ferenc lost his mobile phone. He didn't call us before his visit.
   _____
7 Simona and Pip chatted through the whole meeting. They didn't remember the action points.
   _____
8 Louis didn't start the job immediately. He wasn't able to speak Spanish.
   _____

11 Difficult conversations

Student A

You are going to have two phone conversations. When you are ready to begin, arrange
your seats so that you are sitting back-to-back with your partner.

Conversation 1

1 Before you begin, read your role card carefully.
Make notes if it will help you to role-play the
conversation more effectively.

2 In pairs, role-play your telephone conversation.

> **Role card**
> You are the manager of a small design company. A
> member of your team has not been showing enough
> commitment over the past few months. His / her
> attendance has also been poor. You have spoken to
> him / her about it, and your colleague has promised
> that things will change.
> You have given this member of your team the
> opportunity to prepare a presentation for an important
> new client. The meeting with the client is in a few
> hours' time. Then the phone rings.

Conversation 2

1 Before you begin, read your role card carefully. Make
notes if it will help you to role-play the conversation
more effectively. Think about what you are going to say
before starting.

2 In pairs, role-play your telephone conversation.

> **Role card**
> You work for a major insurance company. You are
> responsible for ordering all the office supplies and
> equipment for the head office.
> This morning, the latest consignment of office
> supplies arrived from PPP, your main supplier. It was
> five days late; some items were missing and others
> were damaged. It is the third time this has happened
> in the last three months.
> You will have to explain the situation to your new
> manager – again. Unfortunately, the last time this
> happened, your manager criticized you for your loyalty
> to PPP.
> Now call PPP and explain the situation.

- -

Student B

You are going to have two phone conversations. When you are ready to begin, arrange
your seats so that you are sitting back-to-back with your partner.

Conversation 1

1 Before you begin, read your role card carefully. Make
notes if it will help you to role-play the conversation
more effectively. Think about what you are going to
say before starting.

2 In pairs, role-play your telephone conversation.

> **Role card**
> You work in a small design company. You enjoy the
> job. However, you are very stressed at the moment
> and it is affecting your attendance and performance at
> work. Your mother / father isn't well and you are
> responsible for looking after her / him. You also have
> to find a new apartment by the end of the month.
> This afternoon, you should be giving a presentation
> to an important new client. You haven't prepared the
> presentation yet, but you planned to do it this
> morning. There are some rough notes and an
> unfinished PowerPoint presentation on your
> computer.
> You have just received an emergency call from your
> mother / father. You have to go and see her / him
> immediately.
> Call your boss and explain that you won't be able to
> come to work today.

Conversation 2

1 Before you begin, read your role card carefully. Make
notes if it will help you to role-play the conversation
more effectively.

2 In pairs, role-play your telephone conversation.

> **Role card**
> You work for PPP, a company which provides high-
> quality office equipment and stationery to a range of
> major companies. Unfortunately, ever since your
> company installed a new computer system, you have
> been having problems tracking orders. This should be
> a short-term problem. However, it has led to some
> delays in dispatching orders.
> Then the phone rings. You know that this customer
> never seems to be happy with your products or your
> service. Unfortunately, he / she is a valuable customer
> and you can't afford to lose the business.

12 Grammar test

1 Report what the following people said to you at a conference.

1 'I may not be able to see you later. Call me on my mobile.'
2 'I've got to give a presentation in five minutes and I can't find my notes!'
3 'Daniel Svoboda gave an excellent presentation this morning.'
4 'I'm thinking of leaving after the next talk.'
5 'Margarita is going to go freelance next month.'
6 'I've just been to an incredibly interesting session.'
7 'I'm sorry, I don't have time to talk. I must get to the next presentation.'
8 'I don't know what your plans are but I've got a great idea.'
9 'I'll tell Martin that I saw you.'
10 'I was running to get to a presentation when I bumped into my ex-boss!'

1 Ana said that *she might not be able to see me later and asked me to call her on her mobile.*
2 Luis told me that _____
3 Peter _____
4 Agnes _____
5 Tanya _____
6 Adam _____
7 Chloe _____
8 Carlos _____
9 Tony _____
10 Joanna _____

2 Write the following questions as reported speech.

1 'What was the best presentation at the conference?'
   She asked me what had been the best presentation at the conference.
2 'How many people were in the audience?'
   _____
3 'What kind of feedback did he get?'
   _____
4 'Do you think he'll stay with his present company?'
   _____
5 'Is he going to talk at the conference in Basle?'
   _____

3 Write the answers to the questions as direct speech.

1 I told her that it had been the one given by Daniel Svoboda.
   It was the one given by Daniel Svoboda.
2 I replied that there had been over 100 people.
   _____
3 I said that I had heard very positive comments from the participants.
   _____
4 I said that I had understood he was thinking about making a move.
   _____
5 I replied that I wasn't sure but I thought he was going to be there.
   _____

12 Presentations – FAQs

1 Discuss these frequently asked questions with your partner. What answers would you give? Note your ideas.

QUESTIONS PRESENTERS FREQUENTLY ASK

1 What do I need to know about my audience?

2 Why do I have to rehearse?

3 Is using PowerPoint always better than using a flipchart?

4 How can I make my voice sound stronger?

5 What should I do when I get to the venue?

6 How can I control my nerves?

2 Match some of the questions with the answers below.

A

It's natural to feel nervous. In fact, if you aren't a bit nervous, something is wrong! Nerves will give you energy. However, to avoid being too nervous:

- Prepare your talk thoroughly and rehearse it as often as you can.
- Visualize yourself giving a successful presentation. Then remember that image when you begin your presentation for real.
- Take some slow, deep breaths before you begin.
- Smile a lot during the presentation (this makes you feel better and look more confident).
- Remember to pause. This gives you time to think – and time to breathe!

B

Knowing who your audience are and what they expect is a way of ensuring that your presentation is appropriate for them.

- Find out who they are and why they are there.
- Ask yourself: what do they know already on the subject, why are they interested, what do they want?
- Keep this information about your audience in mind while you are preparing and giving your presentation.

C

Advantages of PowerPoint:

- It looks professional.
- You can change screens easily.
- You can show images and diagrams, and you can even add video and audio clips.

Advantages of flipcharts:

- They are portable.
- They don't rely on technology.
- They are 'friendly' – more intimate and less formal than the technical options.
- They are flexible.
- You can use them interactively with your audience, noting their opinions and ideas.

D

- Find the power sockets you need for your PowerPoint, etc. and check that all the technology works.
- Ensure that the room is dark enough for your audience to see the screen clearly, but light enough for them to make notes.
- Arrange the room as you want it to be and set up your performance space.
- Make sure that you have everything you need.
- Find the light switch.
- Find out where the toilets are!

3 Do you agree with the advice? Did you think of any extra points? Discuss your ideas in a group of four.

13 Grammar test

1 Complete the sentences with the correct form of the verbs in brackets.

1 We want our shareholders _to enjoy_ (enjoy) the full results of our growth.

2 Small companies often risk _____ (try out) new ideas, which is one reason why they have been so successful in recent years.

3 Fortunately, the company has avoided _____ (go) into liquidation.

4 Business analysts expect _____ (see) a major shake-up in the board of directors.

5 During the Annual General Meeting, the shareholders refused _____ (accept) the proposals of the directors.

6 The chief executive advised the chairperson _____ (reconsider) his decision.

7 The company has given up _____ (attempt) to enter the American market.

8 Imagine, a highly successful advertising agency, has decided _____ (become) a plc.

9 The company has admitted _____ (exaggerate) its profit margins.

10 The spokesperson said that the multinational business didn't deserve _____ (receive) such negative treatment in the press.

2 Look at the following sentences. Tick (✔) the correct ones, cross (✘) the wrong ones, and write the correct form of the verbs.

1 ✘ This is a really complicated situation. I shouldn't have offered ~~taking on~~ _to take on_ extra work.

2 ☐ If Pia continues to make mistakes, she's going to get into trouble.

3 ☐ I think Martina would prefer to work in a much larger company.

4 ☐ I missed to see Alex at the staff party.

5 ☐ The company's recent performance has enabled it expanding its workforce.

6 ☐ James was persuaded to go on the trip in spite of his reservations.

7 ☐ I kept to apply for new jobs, and in the end I was successful.

8 ☐ Carmen suggested finishing the sales report in the morning.

3 Underline the correct option to complete the sentences.

1 Do you intend to continue / continuing to study English after this course?

2 Are you considering to study / studying another language?

3 Have you ever forgotten to go / going to an English lesson?

4 Do you miss to see / seeing friends from your old school?

5 Do you imagine to use / using English in your job?

6 When do you expect to finish / finishing this grammar test?

Now answer the questions about you.

1 _____

2 _____

3 _____

4 _____

5 _____

6 _____

13 Multinationals

1 Work in groups. What do you know about the following multinational corporations? Where are their headquarters? What do they do? What other businesses do they own?

Wal-Mart   Toyota   *Coca-Cola*   Nestlé

Microsoft   Nokia   Shell   **McDonald's**

2 Work in pairs. What advantages do multinationals have over smaller businesses? What disadvantages might they have? Make notes.

3 Read the article.

Circle any information you noted about Wal-Mart in exercise 1.
Underline the ideas you noted in exercise 2.

Multinationals
– giants of the business world

Multinationals can be large ... very large. Take Wal-Mart, for example. Wal-Mart is the world's largest retailer and second-largest corporation with global sales reaching $316 billion in 2006. It is the largest private employer in the US and Mexico. It also owns 2,700 stores in 14 countries in the rest of the world, including India, Brazil, and China. In the UK it operates as ASDA, in Japan as The Seiyu Co., Ltd, and in Mexico as WalMex.

What do these global giants of the business world want? The main objective of any multinational corporation is to expand its operations in the most profitable areas of the world. They want to gain as large a share as possible of the global market, and they want to use all their resources to benefit the businesses in the group.

Clearly, size is important. But what advantages does it bring? Well, their size gives them considerable advantages over smaller corporations. They enjoy the benefits of economies of scale; they can avoid local taxes and duties (for example, a Japanese manufacturer operating in Germany can escape EU tariffs); they can cut their tax bills by declaring their profits in a country with low taxation; they have global access to capital and investment; they can move their business to countries with lower costs; and they can spread their risks by operating in different markets.

But size can also make things difficult. In the way that a huge truck is more difficult to drive than a Mini, so multinationals can be more difficult to control than a small business. And working on such a large scale in different countries can lead to communication problems. They may operate in countries which are politically unstable. They also have to cope with changes in exchange rates which can affect their profitability.

4 In groups, discuss the following opinions.

Multinationals ...

... are too powerful. They have more power than many democratically-elected governments.

... make the world economy more stable and therefore better for everyone.

... damage the environment as they have no real interest in what happens in 'foreign' countries.

... give increased opportunities to workers in the developing world.

14 Grammar test

1 Complete the sentences using the information in brackets and *who*, *which*, or *where*.

1 I have got the exchange rates. (You wanted them by lunchtime.)

   I have got the exchange rates which you wanted by lunchtime.

2 I spoke to Karen Clarke. (She won the Young Entrepreneur of the Year award.)

   I spoke to Karen Clarke _____ *the Young Entrepreneur of the Year award*.

3 Karen has written an e-article. (She explains how she got her original idea in the e-article.)

   Karen has written an e-article _____

4 Peter has cashed the cheque. (I gave it to him.)

   Peter has cashed the cheque _____ him.

5 Hassan Quadi is a business student. (Leon Fassbinder developed the business idea with him.)

   Hassan Quadi is the business student _____

6 They developed the idea at university. (They had enough free time at university.)

   They developed the idea at university _____

2 Complete the sentences with *who* or *that* only if necessary.

1 The website _____ I visited was very uninformative.

2 I admire the guy _____ founded yellow-ice.com.

3 We discussed the idea with the designer _____ we met last week.

4 The overdraft _____ you arranged with the bank isn't large enough.

5 The e-business _____ made phenomenal profits was created by two students.

6 The woman _____ I sat next to at the conference is a successful music producer.

3 Combine these sentences into one sentence using *who* or *which* and the underlined words.

1 Anna del Fiore <u>is only 18.</u> She has become a dot.com millionaire.

   Anna del Fiore, who is only 18, has become a dot.com millionaire.

2 The meeting was a great success. It <u>was held in Prague.</u>

   _____

3 Pawel Dabrowski has just launched his new company. He <u>left business school last year</u>

   _____

4 The company <u>has opened two new branches.</u> It is expanding rapidly.

   _____

5 Ricky Gardiner <u>is now a highly successful young entrepreneur.</u> He wanted to be in a rock band when he was 16.

   _____

6 The website is receiving over two thousand hits per day. It <u>was designed by two teenage sisters.</u>

   _____

14 Managing a budget

1 Work in pairs. Read the text and discuss the question. Make notes.

What advice can you give to students to help them manage their money?

> Are you going to university or college? Are you there now? Have you been there already?
> Well, apart from passing exams, the biggest problem students face is how to survive on a
> budget. Going to university is expensive, so it is important to manage your money carefully.

2 Read the article and tick (✔) any of the advice you thought of in exercise 1.

The student survival guide

☐ **MANAGE YOUR MONEY**

Draw up a weekly budget and then follow it. Calculate how much money you have each month, deduct all your bills and expenses, and you can spend the balance on things you enjoy.

☐ **DO SOME RESEARCH INTO BANKS**

Open an account with a bank that offers the most student benefits. Remember to check the small print – overdrafts can prove very expensive! Arrange for all your monthly bills to be paid by direct debit.

☐ **SHOP INTELLIGENTLY**

You can buy many things second-hand, from reading lamps to books to clothes. If you want to buy a new party dress or jacket, don't go straight to the high street. Wait for the sales, visit factory outlets, and compare prices online.

☐ **TRAVEL CHEAPLY**

You don't need a car. Get a bike or walk. It's good for your pocket and good for your health, too! If you are travelling long distances, do some research to find the cheapest travel option.

☐ **ENTERTAIN YOURSELF**

Learn to cook a few recipes and socialize at home. Rent DVDs rather than going to the cinema.

☐ **WORK!**

Get a part-time job. Bar and restaurant work are good options because you don't have to work during the day. Look for a summer job. By working full time during the holidays, you can save money and help finance your next semester.

3 Work in groups and discuss the questions.

Which tips are the most / least useful?

Is there any useful information you could add to each section?

Did you have any extra ideas for surviving on a budget?

Do you already do any of the things mentioned in the article?

15 Grammar test

1 Report what the people said to you using the verbs in brackets.

1 'You should look at the online job page,' said Alain.

(advise) *Alain advised me to look at the online job page.*

2 'Don't be too negative,' said Nyoko.

(warn) _____

3 'Could you help me with my job application?' said Lucas.

(ask) _____

4 'Remember to keep your CV up to date,' said Alba.

(remind) _____

5 'Meet me at the bar after work,' said Lauren.

(tell) _____

6 'You shouldn't leave before Roger has spoken to you,' said Tomasz.

(advise) _____

2 Write the words in the correct order.

1 CV her he to advised re-write her

He advised her to re-write her CV.

2 the apply to David persuaded for job she

_____

3 online me reminded search Simona to

_____

4 the difficult interview Markus that her be warned would

_____

5 stop he us writing ordered to

_____

6 that she me I situation had to review my told

_____

3 In your notebook report the career advisor's comments with *told* or *advised*.

Thank you for coming to my talk today on how to have a successful job interview.

4 You shouldn't arrive late at the interview.

8 Don't ask too many questions during the interview.

1 You should always rehearse the interview first.

5 You should be enthusiastic about the job on offer.

9 You shouldn't say anything negative about your present boss.

2 You must research the company carefully.

6 Don't ask about the salary and benefits too early in the interview.

10 Be true to yourself.

3 You must select your clothes carefully before you leave home.

7 You should be prepared to talk about your own strengths.

1 *He advised us to rehearse the interview first.*

15 CVs

1 Vicky Adams is applying for a job with a PR company. Read her CV and note anything you feel could be improved. Think about:

layout
contents
too much/not enough information
grammar and spelling

Vicky Adams

25 Claremont Gardens
Manchester
M25 4PD

Profile

I am in the final year of a business studies degree at Manchester Business School. I am very motivated and able to work on my own or as part of a team. I am enthusiastic and able to work to tight deadlines. My communication skills are very good, too.

Major achievements

I have written film and music reviews for the university studnets magazine. I have got experience of working in a PR company (I did a summer job). And finally, I have written a blog for the last three years which everyone says is interesting and entertaining.

Experience

Sports teacher
15 August 2006 – 12 September 2006 Sherwood summer school
I had to organize sports activities for foreign students including football, swimming, tennis, inline skating, ice hockey, skateboarding, running, table tennis, athletics, etc. I gained a lot of useful experience in motivating and dealing with people.

Admininistrative assistant
7 July 2007 – 27 August 2007 Clarke and Wells
This was a vacation job for a PR company.
I have done general office work including answering the telephone, photocopying, and filing. I also did proofreading and gained a lot of really useful experience.

Education

Manchester Business School, UK
I'm studying lots of courses which provide valuable skills and knowledge.

Brighton High School, Sussex, UK
3 A levels
English literature (Grade B)
History (Grade B) Economics (Grade A)
7 GCSEs
History, Geography, English, French, Mathematics, Food technology.

Other skills

I have eccellent computer skills.
I can ride a horse.
I have a clean driver's licence.

Interests

In my free time I enjoy listening to live music in clubs and going out with friends. I love doing most sports but especially football, squash, tennis, hockey, and running. I also love winter sports such as snowboarding. I like travelling and I try to get away most summers. Recently I have visited Hungry, Poland and the Czech Republic. Next year I hope to go to Australia,

References

I can ask people to write references if you want them.

2 Compare your ideas with a partner.

Grammar tests key

Unit 1

1 2 'm finishing
3 start
4 finish
5 'm working
6 passes
7 deal
8 liaise
9 'm preparing
10 have
11 'm putting in
12 love

2 2 does ... get; arrives; 's having
3 Is ... working; don't know; make
4 are ... living / do ... live; 'm renting; hope
5 are ... doing; 're making
6 does ... think; says; don't believe

3 2 ✓
3 ✗ Do you want ...
4 ✗ ... is aiming ...
5 ✓
6 ✓
7 ✗ ... usually eat
8 ✓

Unit 2

1 2 went
3 talked
4 were chatting
5 graduated
6 took
7 travelled
8 did
9 was working
10 decided
11 wanted
12 was feeling
13 got up
14 started
15 was stretching
16 heard
17 turned
18 saw
19 was doing
20 was finishing
21 set up

2 2 while / when
3 when
4 while / when
5 when
6 While / When

3 2 was
3 was going
4 saw
5 was
6 seemed
7 were you talking
8 was talking
9 went
10 Did you accept
11 decided

Unit 3

1 2 Have you gone
3 haven't.
4 Have you seen
5 been crying?
6 's just got back
7 's left
8 've been sitting
9 've noticed
10 've been talking
11 haven't decided

2 2 c 3 f 4 b 5 d 6 e

3 b 've been speaking / 've spoken; 've been trying
c 've written; 've been working; haven't finished
d 've done
e have; 've been doing
f haven't; 've been preparing

Unit 4

1 2 shouldn't have criticized
3 should have attended
4 shouldn't have used
5 shouldn't have chatted
6 should have taken

2 2 'll have to
3 didn't have to
4 had to
5 had to go
6 didn't have to
7 shouldn't have

Unit 5

1 2 'll be free
3 'll send it again
4 'm going to apply for it
5 's going to ask for a promotion
6 'll get you
7 's going to do it
8 's going to leave

2 1 ✓
2 ✗ ... it will have ...
3 ✗ ... 's going to meet ...
4 ✗ ... 'll explain
5 ✗ ... will you know
6 ✗ ... 'll have

3 2 will be able to work
3 will have to start
4 won't be able to access
5 will be able to meet
6 will have to take on

Unit 6

1 2 can't be
3 can't want
4 must be
5 must feel
6 can't belong
7 must know
8 can't come
9 must enjoy
10 must have

2 3 They can't be right. / They must be wrong.
4 He may / could be depressed.
5 She must be working too much.
6 There must be a fault on the line.
7 He may / could take a gap year.
8 It can't be my phone.

3 2 can't   3 could   4 must   5 can't

Unit 7

1 2 were studied
3 was claimed
4 were held
5 was reported
6 was discovered
7 had been invested
8 was forced
9 was suspended
10 were arrested

2 2 will be completed
3 Were children exploited / Have children been exploited
4 are being reviewed
5 was founded
6 have been increased
7 has been used / is used
8 will be consumed

3 2 ... was being listened to by a large audience.
3 ... are being given the opportunity to buy shares in its company by Cafédirect.
4 ... must be written by my manager.
5 ... might be bought by the company later this year.
6 ... should have been given by Markus.

Unit 8

1 2 g 3 c 4 h 5 d 6 e 7 a 8 b

2 2 get, might take
3 'll be, don't give
4 see, 'll definitely tell
5 won't drive, pay
6 will she do, doesn't get
7 will improve, go
8 're able to prove, will pay

Unit 9

1 2 got, had already discussed
3 decided, had mainly focused
4 had sponsored, revealed
5 met, revealed, had thought of

6 had already launched, founded
7 decided, had rejected
8 got, had started

2 2 c I had failed ...
3 h I hadn't been able to get to sleep ...
4 g I had fixed ...
5 b he had used ...
6 e I had missed ...
7 a I had been ...
8 d the server had gone down

3 2 hadn't attended an overseas trade fair before.
3 had always wanted to work abroad.
4 he had met her at a conference the year before.
5 had worked in Tokyo before.
6 had just gone out.

Unit 10

1 2 must have gone out
3 can't have worked
4 must have finished
5 can't have tidied
6 can't have got
7 can't have talked
8 must have exceeded

3 1 She must have been delayed by the traffic.
2 He must have had a headache.
3 He must have gone to get a drink.
4 He must have worked late last night.
5 She must have been looking for jobs.

Unit 11

1 2 f 3 h 4 b 5 a 6 g 7 e 8 c

2 2 would you have done, 'd continued
3 had been, would never have happened
4 he have won, 'd been
5 wouldn't have developed, hadn't done
6 'd met, wouldn't have upset
7 would have gone, 'd told
8 had been, wouldn't have flown

3 2 We would have got to the meeting on time if there hadn't been a traffic jam.
3 Jan would have got the order if he'd listened closely to the customer.
4 Michael would have got the job as a translator if he hadn't failed the exam.
5 Karen would have got the job if she'd had better communication skills.
6 Ferenc would have called us before his visit if he hadn't lost his mobile phone.

7 Simona and Pip would have remembered the action points if they hadn't chatted through the whole meeting.

8 Louis would have started the job immediately if he'd been able to speak Spanish.

Unit 12

1 2 Luis told me that he had got to give a presentation in five minutes and he couldn't find his notes.

3 Peter said that Daniel Svoboda had given an excellent presentation that morning.

4 Agnes told me that she was thinking of leaving after the following talk.

5 Tanya said that Margarita was going to go freelance the following month.

6 Adam told me that he had just been to an incredibly interesting session.

7 Chloe said that she was sorry, she didn't have time to talk. She had to get to the next presentation.

8 Carlos told me that he didn't know what my plans were but he'd got a great idea.

9 Tony said that he would tell Martin that he'd seen me.

10 Joanna told me that she had been running to get to a presentation when she had bumped into her ex-boss.

2 2 She asked me how many people had been in the audience.

3 She asked me what kind of feedback he had got.

4 She asked me if I thought he would stay with his present company.

5 She asked me if he was going to talk at the conference in Basle.

3 2 There were over 100 people.

3 I heard very positive comments from the participants.

4 I understood that he is thinking about making a move.

5 I'm not sure but I think he's going to be there.

Unit 13

1
2	trying out	7	attempting
3	going	8	to become
4	to see	9	exaggerating
5	to accept	10	to receive
6	to reconsider		

2
2	✓	6	✓
3	✓	7	✗ applying
4	✗ seeing	8	✓
5	✗ to expand		

3
1	to continue	4	seeing
2	studying	5	using
3	to go	6	to finish

Unit 14

1 2 who won

3 in which she explains how she got her original idea

4 which I gave (to)

5 with whom Leon Fassbinder developed the business idea. / who Leon Fassbinder developed the business idea with

6 where they had enough free time.

2 2 who   3 –   4 –   5 that   6 –

3 2 The meeting, which was held in Prague, was a great success.

3 Pawel Dabrowski, who left business school last year, has just launched his new company.

4 The company, which has opened two new branches, is expanding rapidly.

5 Ricky Gardiner, who is now a highly successful young entrepreneur, wanted to be in a rock band when he was 16.

6 The website, which was designed by two teenage sisters, is receiving over two thousand hits per day.

Unit 15

1 2 Nyoko warned me not to be too negative.

3 Lucas asked me to help him with his job application.

4 Alba reminded me to keep my CV up to date.

5 Lauren told me to meet her at the bar after work.

6 Tomasz advised me not to leave before Roger had spoken to me.

2 2 She persuaded David to apply for the job.

3 Simona reminded me to search online.

4 Markus warned her that the interview would be difficult.

5 He ordered us to stop writing.

6 She told me that I had to review my situation.

3 2 He advised / told us to research the company carefully.

3 He advised / told us to select our clothes carefully before we left home.

4 He advised / told us not to arrive late at the interview.

5 He advised / told us to be enthusiastic about the job on offer.

6 He advised / told us not to ask about the salary and benefits too early in the interview.

7 He advised / told us to be prepared to talk about our own strengths.

8 He advised / told us not to ask too many questions during the interview.

9 He advised / told us not to say anything negative about our present boss.

10 He advised / told us to be true to ourselves.